CHOOSE YOUR PATH!

ATTACK ON TITAN

ADVENTURE

THE HUNT FOR THE FEMALE TITAN

BY **TOMOYUKI FUJINAMI**

Illustrated by **Ryosuke Fuji and Toru Yoshii**

ATTACK ON TITAN CREATED BY **HAJIME ISAYAMA**

Prologue

This world belongs to the Titans.

Reduced to mere fodder for the giant creatures, humanity built three massive walls, and within them established a fragile peace and order. This peace lasted for a century, and humanity forgot the terror that waited beyond the walls.

But five years ago, in the year 845, the first wall, Wall Maria, was destroyed when the Colossus Titan appeared. Humanity lost a third of its territory and twenty percent of its population, and remembered their fear of the Titans. They remembered that they were little more than caged livestock.

Five years after that attack, the Colossus Titan reappeared near Trost District, the southernmost point of the second wall, Wall Rose. It destroyed the main gate, and Titans began to massacre the populace. Humanity had learned from its experience five years earlier, but the Titans were simply too powerful. Even the freshly minted soldiers of the Training Corps were mustered and thrown into the awful fight that became known as the Battle of Trost.

This battle concluded with the retreat of the Titans and the successful blockage of the demolished gate. This was the first recorded human victory over the Titans, but it came at a tremendous cost. Countless soldiers lay dead on the field, including many young trainees who hadn't yet even been inducted as full soldiers.

And so we come to the year 850. The fight is not over.

This is an *Attack on Titan* game book.

You, the reader, will enter the world of *Attack on Titan* to fight and survive. You are the protagonist of this book. The choices you make will determine what happens in the story.

You are a member of the 104th Training Corps, a nameless soldier who has survived the Battle of Trost. Now that your hellish baptism by fire is behind you, you must choose your path in the military. Will you join the Survey Corps, the group that ventures into the dangerous world beyond the walls to confront the Titans?

If so, a merciless destiny awaits you. This world is unfeeling and cruel. If you make the wrong choice, you will be punished with immediate destruction. The Titans you will face on the battlefield are overwhelming. And they may not be your only enemies this time.

However, with calm judgment and appropriate action, you can survive. You may even contribute to the human military's cherished objective—the capture of a Titan. Indeed... you may even save friends who seemed fated to die.

If you're ready, turn the page and start at section 1.

The Titans pour into the city, one after another. The creatures are easy to spot because they loom over even the tallest buildings.

This is Trost District. The town was supposed to be safe behind its walls—but suddenly the Colossus Titan appeared and destroyed the town gate, letting in this flood of man-eating monsters.

You are a member of the 104th Training Corps. You've spent the last three years learning to fight, and today was to be the day you were inducted as a full member of the armed forces. You couldn't have imagined that this was how your day of celebration would turn out. You and your fellow trainees have been thrown into the battle.

Your enemies are numerous and massive. Your friends, including the more experienced soldiers, are killed one after another, devoured by Titans. You are wracked with exhaustion; you can hardly move. You're almost out of gas for your Vertical Maneuvering Equipment, as well.

That's when the black-haired boy appears. You know his uniform; he's one of the other trainees. You feel a rush of relief—until his body begins to grow in size, and he becomes a Titan himself!

What do you do?

More Titans? You run away as fast as you can (Go to **2**)

A human who can turn into a Titan? You're going to bring him down! (Go to **3**)

Work with this transforming Titan to fight nearby enemies (Go to **4**)

This is how the adventure proceeds: when you've decided what to do, turn the page and go to the number indicated.

●2

On the battlefield, when you let fear take control of you and rob you of rational judgment, the only possible outcome is death.

You fail in your attempt to run—a giant hand grabs you, and you are eaten by a Titan. (Go to **5**)

●3

You launch yourself at the Titan, using vertical maneuvering to help you move. You can sense a humanlike intelligence in this Titan's eyes. You remember your comrade, Eren, and hesitate. The Titan roars. From anger, or sorrow? But then he begins to rampage, as if he's just another monster. Is it because you didn't trust him? Or is this what was inside him all along?

His face looms in your vision, and his mouth is wide open… (Go to **5**)

●4

You remind yourself—you remember that this creature was one of your comrades. You're sure he's different from the Titans who attack and eat humans.

The Titan looks down at you, intelligence and emotion in his eyes. He'll be a stalwart ally. With him on your side, you can beat the other Titans!

Before you know it, the scene before you has changed. The black-haired Titan is walking along, carrying a boulder almost as big as he is. Your comrades are sacrificing themselves to protect him. People you know, people you care about, are among the dead. And yet, the Titan must be protected. He is humanity's very hope for survival...

Soldiers drop like flies. The black-haired Titan steps over their corpses, moving ever forward.

You, too, join the fight to defend him... (Go to **5**)

● **5**

You open your eyes. It was all a dream. You're soaked with sweat.

It all starts to come back. You're in the Garrison, and all the things you just dreamed about are over.

The Battle of Trost was some days ago. It was a brutal fight with the Titans, and many soldiers died, including no small number of your brothers and sisters in arms from the 104th Training Corps. After the battle, you were assigned to help with corpse retrieval duty in the city. You remember all too well the horrifying state many of your friends were in. Ever since then, you've had nightmares almost every night. And it's not just you. They seem to afflict a large number of your comrades.

The dream you just had... may not have been something you actually experienced. Actual memories are so easily confused with things you've only heard about.

You know it's a fact that Eren Yeager, who was in the same class as you, turned into a Titan, and you know that was the key to humanity's victory. You know it's true, but it's not an easy story to believe. Deep in your heart, you're afraid of Eren, and maybe that's what led to your dream… (Go to **6**)

●6 Instructions

You remember. You are part of the 104th Training Corps, stationed at the Wall Rose South District training camp.

This posting at the southernmost border of human territory is what got you involved in the Battle of Trost a few days ago. Humanity snatched victory from the jaws of the Titans, but not before a great many soldiers had sacrificed themselves. The fact that you survived may be nothing more than luck…

You ponder your dream. Is Eren not really a friend? No. You don't want to start thinking like that. But suppose there were other humans who could turn into Titans… Are there any guarantees that they would be allies, too?

****

How to Use this Book

This is an *Attack on Titan* adventure.

You take on the role of a member of the 104th Training Corps and, along with your classmates including Eren, Mikasa, and Armin, plumb the mystery of one Titan in particular.

You are the protagonist of this book. It explores an alternate history of *Attack on Titan*: What if you had been there? What if you had been a part of it all?

The Battle Report Sheet

On page 12 of this book you will find a Battle Report Sheet.

When you find important clues in the story, or if you obtain an item, write it down here. You may wish to use a pencil so you can erase what you've written.

Of course, you aren't required to use this sheet. You can record things on a separate sheet of paper or in a notebook—or, if you're confident in your powers of recall, you can fight without writing anything down.

You are a member of the 104th Training Corps. You're about the same age as your classmates, such as Eren and Mikasa, between 15 and 17 years old. You can pick your own name and gender, or you can leave them undetermined.

List of Comrades and "Affinity"

The Battle Report Sheet lists your brothers and sisters in arms— your classmates in the 104th Training Corps, as well as other soldiers on the battlefield with you. It doubles as a casualty register. If you see one of these people die in battle, or if you receive word of their death, mark them dead on this page.

You can also have a degree of **Affinity** with certain other characters. To start with, your **Affinity** with each other character is zero. It may change due to actions you take during the story. You may wish to use tally marks to keep track of your Affinity.

The Female Titan and the "Kill Count"

During the story, you may eventually encounter a creature known as the Female Titan. The **Kill Count** represents how many humans this Titan has killed. It starts at zero. If, while reading, you see the instruction **"increase the Kill Count,"** then add to the number on the Battle Report Sheet.

Keeping the **Kill Count** to a minimum (that is, avoiding human casualties) will be a primary concern for you. This number has another meaning as well, but that's for you to find out.

Puzzles Hidden Throughout the Book

Throughout this book you will encounter puzzles, such as codes and hidden words or numbers. Solving these puzzles may give you a chance to change your circumstances—or your destiny.

But this is the world of *Attack on Titan*, and these may not be letters and numbers as you recognize them. They are shown abstractly, demanding your powers of discernment and your ability to observe what is going on. If you solve the puzzles, it means you've taken good stock of the situation on the ground, or have acted exceptionally.

This section will not explain exactly what form these puzzles will take. That is for you to discover on your own.

Alternate Endings

This book depicts the 104th Training Corps' progression into the ranks, as well as the 57th Expedition Outside the Walls and the Battle of Stohess District, seen in volumes 5-8 of the *Attack on Titan* manga. In short, it covers the so-called "Female Titan Arc."

There are a number of possible endings.

Depending on your choices, you may receive a worse ending than that in the manga: humanity may be defeated, or characters who survived in the original version may die.

On the other hand, if you manage to survive the fight, you may get different endings based on your **Affinity** with various characters.

There is even the possibility that, if you solve the puzzles and truly distinguish yourself, the story may develop or conclude differently from the original; you may even be able to save your friends from a brutal death.

Everything depends on your choices.

Choose so that you are left with no regrets.

Are you ready? Then turn the page.

(Beginning on the next page, you will find the Battle Report Sheet, as well as Current Publicly Available Information that you may wish to know about this world. The story resumes with section 8 on page 16.)

SURVEY CORPS

CAPTAIN
LEVI

AFFINITY

PETRA RAL

GUNTHER
SCHULTZ

DIETER
NESS

AFFINITY

HANGE ZOË

OLUO
BOZADO

ELD JINN

LUKE SISS

104th TRAINING CORPS

AFFINITY

SASHA
BLOUSE

AFFINITY

JEAN
KIRSTEIN

MARCO
BOTT

CONNIE
SPRINGER

KRISTA
LENZ

AFFINITY

YMIR

REINER
BRAUN

BERTOLT
HOOVER

MARK THE DEAD WITH AN X.

BATTLE REPORT SHEET

YOUR NAME:

BATTLE NOTES: CLUES, ITEMS, ETC.

KEY NUMBERS   A [   ]   Y [   ]   R [   ]

FEMALE TITAN

MIKASA ACKERMAN

EREN YEAGER

ARMIN ARLERT

ANNIE LEONHART

(KILL COUNT)

●7 Current Publicly Available Information

On Titans

Titans eat humans: that is, you. They vary in height, from around two meters to more than 17 meters. Most Titans are "Normal Types" that appear to seek out and devour humans primarily by instinct. It is unknown whether Titans are intelligent, but they have never been seen to use tools, their movements are slow, and they are incapable of complex physical operations.

However, a certain number of so-called **"Abnormals"** exist as well. This term covers a wide range of types, but the common factor is that their behavior is unpredictable. Some Abnormals are capable of quick movement, or behave as though intelligent.

Titan Weaknesses and Fighting Titans

Titan body temperatures are exceptionally high, and they possess powerful regenerative abilities. If they lose a limb, or even their head, they will regenerate it within one to two minutes. The only way to kill a Titan is to deal severe damage to the nape of its neck. Currently, humanity does not possess artillery capable of precisely targeting that specific spot. For this reason, we have a developed a battle tactic in which one maneuvers behind the Titan and delivers a deep cut to the nape of the neck. This is made possible by **Vertical Maneuvering Equipment**.

The Various Corps

The **Training Corps** to which you presently belong is where the future members of every branch of the military receive their basic training. Those who survive the three years of grueling preparation then enter regular service in one of the following three branches.

The Garrison: Each town within the walls has its own unit of Garrison forces to protect the people. Most soldiers end up here.

The Military Police Brigade: Oversees the populace and preserves public order under the command of the king. They are the elites; only the most exceptional trainees are allowed to join them.

The Survey Corps: They make dangerous forays beyond the walls to discover what's out there. They get practical experience fighting Titans, but casualties are high.

Eren Yeager – The Boy who can Become a Titan

Eren Yeager is one of your classmates in the Training Corps. During the Battle of Trost, he used his ability to turn into a Titan to lead humanity to victory. But how he became a Titan—the reason and the principle by which it works—is unknown, and Eren himself claims not to understand it. Indeed, there is much that isn't clear about the Titans as a species.

During his transformation, Eren didn't appear to be in complete control of himself, and although he eventually succeeded in controlling his Titan body, it was not until after he had gone on a rampage and attacked some of your comrades. Eren is the only person confirmed to be able to turn into a Titan. It is not currently known whether other people with similar powers exist.

(When you have reviewed this information, go to **8**. You may refer to this page at any time.)

●8 After the Battle of Trost

You think back on the vicious Battle of Trost.

The fight was hideously one-sided, with Titans pressing in all around. Even the more experienced soldiers were dropping like flies, with the guard unit in tatters. The one silver lining was that with their sacrifice, the soldiers bought time for the people to safely evacuate.

In the midst of this chaos, a boy from the 104th Training Corps, Eren Yeager, transformed into a Titan. It allowed him to save his friends from danger, but even Eren didn't seem to know how he had done it. When Commander Pixis arrived with reinforcements, he came up with a bold plan to use the Titan Eren as a "living weapon" to retake Trost District. The operation cost many lives, but ultimately succeeded. Eren, in his Titan form, used a massive boulder to plug the hole in the town gate.

This was humanity's first victory against the Titans.

Eren, however, was not hailed as a hero. The other soldiers regarded him as something weird and dangerous; he was put to a court-martial, where some even suggested that he should be executed and his body dissected for science.

Thanks to the quick thinking and intervention of the Survey Corps, including its commander, Erwin, Eren was spared execution and was instead released into the custody of the Survey Corps. Or so you've heard…

Now, where are you after the Battle of Trost?

With Eren in "Squad Levi" of the Survey Corps (Go to **12**)

With your friends at the army headquarters in Trost District (Go to **18**)

"Eren…" one of your comrades says. "He was about to kill Mikasa, wasn't he?"

There are rumors about the incident: they say that when Eren transformed into a Titan, he lost his sanity and began going berserk.

Armin doesn't deny it. "It's true, he was. But in the end, he found his human heart again. Eren led us to victory." Armin should know. He was there. "Not to mention, he never actually killed any of his allies. There's a big difference between the potential to kill and actually killing. If he had accidentally caused any casualties, I'll bet even Commander Erwin and the others wouldn't have been able to cover for him at the tribunal."

Everyone nods. This makes sense to them.

You feel a rush of admiration. Armin is a smart young man. Yet at the same time, you can't help feeling like his story has a certain

detachment. If Eren had "accidentally caused any casualties," what would Armin be saying now?

The boy glances at somebody. You follow his gaze and see Annie. She's trying to look disinterested, but you think she was quite engaged in Armin's story.

(Return **to the map at 20** and choose a new destination.)

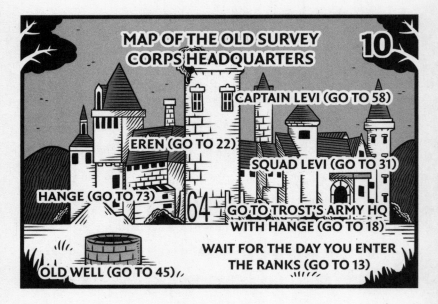

MAP OF THE OLD SURVEY CORPS HEADQUARTERS

CAPTAIN LEVI (GO TO 58)

EREN (GO TO 22)

SQUAD LEVI (GO TO 31)

HANGE (GO TO 73)

64

GO TO TROST'S ARMY HQ WITH HANGE (GO TO 18)

WAIT FOR THE DAY YOU ENTER THE RANKS (GO TO 13)

OLD WELL (GO TO 45)

●11

You're at the old Survey Corps headquarters, where you've come with Squad Leader Hange. You've received special permission to enter, partly on the basis of being a classmate of Eren's.

The former Survey Corps base is a dilapidated building located well away from the city center or any of the villages. Levi and the other members of his squad operating here are cautious, but regard you with a certain friendliness. Maybe they're interested in you because you have real experience fighting Titans, even though you're just a trainee.

This building has been out of use for a long time. Yet despite its age, the interior is sparkling. Apparently the first thing Captain Levi did was to order a thorough cleaning. Maybe part of being a top-level soldier is doing a good job at even the most mundane tasks.

(Consult section 10, the map of the old Survey Corps headquarters, on the previous page, and follow it to where you want to go.)

●12

Your actions in the Battle of Trost got the attention of Captain Levi and the other members of the Survey Corps, and, combined with the fact that you were a classmate of Eren's, you're granted special dispensation to work with Squad Levi. You aren't a full member of the Survey Corps—consider it an apprenticeship.

The two of you go to the former Survey Corps headquarters, a dilapidated structure located well away from the city center or any of the villages. Supposedly, it's a safe place for Eren to lie low for a while. Whether it's meant to be safe for Eren, or for those around him, is hard to tell...

Your duties begin with cleaning this long-unused building. The sight of the more experienced members of the Survey Corps, elite soldiers all, putting on aprons and bandannas and doing housekeeping is very strange. Captain Levi, often called the strongest soldier in human history, has turned his undivided attention to cleaning up this building. You can tell top-level soldiers are different from other people even when they're doing the most mundane tasks.

(Consult section 10, the map of the old Survey Corps headquarters, on the previous page, and follow it to where you want to go.)

You can simply wait here, helping Captain Levi and the other squad members, until the day you become a full soldier. If you do, go to **56**. Careful: you won't be able to return to this map.

If there's anything else you still want to do, return to **the map at 10** and choose a new destination.

●14 **Dead End**

You have died.

Were you killed by a Titan? If so, then if you were lucky; your companions might have seen you die, and will report it so you can be registered among the fatalities. If you're even luckier, they might be able to collect your body, or at least some personal effects, and return them to your remaining family. Many who perish fighting the Titans don't even get that.

Or were you killed by something else? You may accept your death and rest from your struggle. If so, close the book now.

But… if you have the strength of heart to challenge the terrifying Titans once again, there is a way.

Return to the point immediately before your death and try again. If you can't remember where you died, return to **1** or **8**. You come to, not quite able to remember what happened, but feeling that you had a strange dream.

Alternatively, you can start again as another trainee (that is, another member of the 104th Training Corps, which has received word of your demise). In this case, reset your Affinity with each character to zero, but keep any flags and secret numbers you've obtained. The things you achieved before your death benefit the new "you."

What happens to characters other than you who have died, as well as the Kill Count, will depend on where you restart from.

Now, turn the page and return to your fight.

●15

"Yeah." Your words evoke a sad smile from Armin. "You're right. Why would I doubt my comrades? Maybe the fatigue is getting to me."

(Increase your **Affinity with Armin** by 1 and go to **95**.)

●16

"Wh-What makes you bring her up?" Bertolt seems unusually edgy.

Reiner, however, looks thoughtful. He seems to be choosing his words carefully. "Hm. Annie Leonhart? We're not very close, but I'm confident she's a good soldier. I remember she threw me in combat training once, like I was light as a feather."

Maybe it's that memory that makes his shoulders slump. Reiner is no slouch himself in hand-to-hand combat, so Annie must be quite a fighter. Bertolt adds, almost as though apologizing for her, "She's... Sh-She's not a bad person. She keeps her comrades at arm's length, but I think she just isn't very social..." (If you ask them what unit they're going to join, go to **54**. If you go somewhere else, return to **the map at 20**.)

●17

If you were with Eren after the Battle of Trost, go to **39**. Otherwise, go to **49**.

●18

You are at the army headquarters in the heart of Trost District.

After the Titan Eren succeeded in blocking the ruined gate with the huge boulder, the fixed guns on top of Trost's walls along with the efforts of the Survey Corps succeeded in mopping up the remaining Titans in the city.

You may be free from the immediate threat of the Titans, but the city remains in shambles, and the citizens can't yet resume their normal lives. The army headquarters miraculously survived the battle unscathed, and has been turned into an impromptu base. The survivors of your 104th Training Corps are here, too, helping out with whatever the army needs done. But it's really just a way of passing the time...

(**Look at the map of Trost District army headquarters, section 20, on the next page.** Decide who you want to see and then go to that number. Or you can simply wait for the day you become a full soldier, in which case go to **19**.)

●19

You can simply wait here with the other members of the 104th Training Corps until the day you become a full soldier. If you do, go to **57**. Careful: you won't be able to return to this map. If there's anything else you still want to do, return to **the map at 20** and choose a new destination.

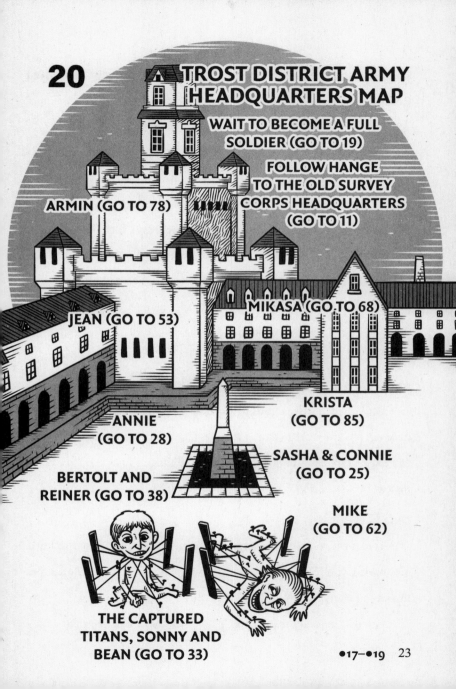

20

TROST DISTRICT ARMY HEADQUARTERS MAP

WAIT TO BECOME A FULL
SOLDIER (GO TO 19)

FOLLOW HANGE
TO THE OLD SURVEY
CORPS HEADQUARTERS
(GO TO 11)

ARMIN (GO TO 78)

MIKASA (GO TO 68)

JEAN (GO TO 53)

KRISTA
(GO TO 85)

ANNIE
(GO TO 28)

SASHA & CONNIE
(GO TO 25)

BERTOLT AND
REINER (GO TO 38)

MIKE
(GO TO 62)

THE CAPTURED
TITANS, SONNY AND
BEAN (GO TO 33)

You remove your familiar trainee's uniform and don the "Dual Rose" of a Garrison soldier. In light of your experiences in this area, you're assigned to the unit defending Trost District.

There's a great deal to do, from the maintenance of the walltop guns to the repair of the damaged city. The work is hard, but there's no danger of Titans attacking this place; the days go by in peace.

Before you know it, it's been a month. The army officially announces that the Survey Corps will be making an expedition outside the walls.

Trost District was once an important base for these forays, but with its gate rendered useless, it can no longer fill that role. The Survey Corps will be using the eastern district of Karanes as their launching point this time. You wonder if those among your comrades who joined the Survey Corps will be all right…

You've been assigned to guard duty atop the walls. You cast your gaze out toward what's beyond them. Of course, from this distance, you can't see so much as the faintest shadow of the Survey Corps far, far to the east. (Go to 216)

You meet with your classmate, Eren Yeager. Another soldier is monitoring your conversation, as a guard, and you've been warned not to ask about anything inappropriate.

You take a good look at Eren, but he still looks like a normal young man to you. Can he really turn into a Titan…?

"Oh, it's you," Eren says. "How's everyone doing?"

He seems to be asking after your other classmates. You tell him what you can, given the gaze of the soldier standing nearby. When you inform him that several people he knows are safe, Eren seems very relieved. He isn't exactly under house arrest here, let alone tied up in a jail cell somewhere, but neither does he seem to have true freedom of movement.

"I sleep in a basement room. I think the idea is that if I accidentally turn into a Titan in my sleep, it'll be too confined for me to do anything." He laughs uneasily. Eren doesn't seem to have suffered any external injuries, but he appears subdued. No doubt there's a lot on his mind.

Finally he says, "I know how this looks, but I've become a real member of the Survey Corps." He pauses, then says, "You know, I wonder what everyone else is going to do about their future. After what happened… I wouldn't blame anyone for not wanting to join the Survey Corps anymore."

(Return to **the map at 10** and choose a new destination.)

●23

"I picked this team myself," Levi says. "They've fought Titans outside the walls. They've survived hellish conditions, time and again."

Levi is a man of few words, but you can tell how much he's trusted.

(If you ask him something else, go to **58**. Otherwise, return to **the map at 10** and choose a new destination. The captain is a busy man.)

●24

"In the well, we did experiments on Eren's ability to turn into a Titan," he says. "But no matter how many times he bit his own hand, he couldn't do it. But look… We took him out of the well and were having a break, drinking some tea, and all of a sudden his arm—just his arm—turned into a Titan arm. When we asked him about it afterward, it didn't sound like he did it on purpose. According to Squad Leader Hange, he was trying to pick up a spoon or something…"

Gunther scratches his own cheek uncomfortably.

"We were pretty panicked, so yeah… We didn't ask nicely. Weapons out." He pauses, then says, "We did wrong. He bit that hand til it flowed with blood. It must've hurt."

You notice something on Gunther's palm as he speaks to you: a scar, the imprint of teeth. It must be their way of apologizing to Eren.

(Return to **the map at 10** and choose a new destination.)

Your classmates Sasha and Connie are standing and talking together. They're discussing the units they want to join, a decision you'll all have to make soon. Both of them were at the top of your class, so they could choose the Military Police Brigade if they want to.

"I'm definitely thinking about the MPs," Connie says. "I was planning to join the Survey Corps like Eren. But when we had to fight the Titans for real, I was just... I was so scared. And the Military Police Brigade is supposed to be the elite of the elite. If I could get in there, it would make my mom proud."

"You're right," Sasha says. "The Military Police are a good choice. I hear they get good food, too. They don't have to live on potatoes. They get meat and everything..."

As enthusiastic as both of them sound, their expressions are dark. They seem to be wondering if the MPs are really the right choice.

(Return to **the map at 20** and choose a new destination.)

●26

"I wouldn't lose to the likes of him," Mikasa mutters. There's no question that her fighting abilities are superb. She might even be the equal of Captain Levi... (Go to **69**)

"Hmph. I liked the look in his eyes when he declared that he was going to destroy all the Titans." Levi stares into space for a second. "He might make a good soldier… but he does have a Titan within him. If he can't control it, then I will bury him. That's all there is to it."

(If you ask him something else, go to **58**. Otherwise, return to **the map at 10** and choose a new destination. The captain is a busy man.)

●28

You spot Annie Leonhart and call out to her. With her golden hair and sense of style, there's no question Annie is attractive, but her aquiline nose and sharp features make her intimidating as well. She has a hard look in her eyes and doesn't seem to want to get close to people.

Even in training, she was taciturn and never very expressive. Neither did she seem especially close to anyone else in the unit. When you call her name, she turns toward you with a look of annoyance.

"Oh, it's you," she says disinterestedly. "You want something?"

Ask which unit she plans to join (Go to **55**)

Ask her to teach you martial arts (Go to **43**)

●29

Hange's explanation is long and technical, and most of it goes over your head. The following points, however, sink in.

"Titans eventually stop moving when they're totally cut off from sunlight. How long it takes varies from Titan to Titan.

"The Survey Corps has never before succeeded in actually capturing a Titan like this and subjecting it to observation and experiments. If we can keep gathering data, it could give us a huge advantage in our struggle against the Titans."

You gather that this is the first time anyone has managed to demonstrate the truth of the point about sunlight. You have to admit, you're impressed. If the Survey Corps can continue to study their two captives, there's a lot they can learn about the formerly inscrutable Titans. You might start to find out who your enemies really are, and that thought gives you hope.

"Anyway, I've got to get back to my experiments!"

Hange is finally done talking.

(If this is the first time you've read this passage, increase your **Affinity with Hange** by 1. Return to either **the map at 10 or the map at 20**, depending on how you got here, and choose a new destination.)

●30

Mikasa is lost for words. She stares at you, her eyes wide.

Finally, she says, "I know that. But I should have done better. The failure was mine." (Go to **69**)

The Survey Corps Special Operations Squad, informally known as Squad Levi, has four members. They are all specially chosen, distinguished soldiers even within the elite ranks of the Survey Corps. You salute; they return the gesture and introduce themselves. You find them surprisingly friendly.

Petra, the only woman in the squad, is the first to speak to you. "You're from the 104th Training Corps, aren't you? Eren's classmate."

"Eren's group…?" Eld and Gunther, two men, mutter together. They don't seem to like this news.

"Feh. So you're friends with that prissy little brat? Just mind you don't get in the way, rookie," the final member, Oluo, says threateningly.

You…

Ask about Levi, Eren, and Hange (Go to **87**)

Take umbrage at Oluo's tone (Go to **32**)

"So you want to know why I said that?" Oluo scoffs. "I don't think a greenhorn like you would get it." Maybe he thinks he sounds cynical. "I'm not a nice enough guy to just spill the beans for you, either. Have a think and figure it out for yourself."

Petra breaks in. "Stop that, Oluo. You're not doing yourself any favors. You never used to talk like that. If you think you sound like Captain Levi, you don't at all. Remember that time we were on horseback and you were blathering away dramatically and bit your tongue?"

This exchange clarifies things for you. These people greatly respect Levi, and are very focused on him. Still… maybe Oluo's a little strange.

"Heh heh! Petra," he says. "You're practically hen-pecking me. I know we're in the same squad, but I'm not ready to make you my wife just yet!"

"I wish you'd bitten your tongue off and died from blood loss..."

You wonder: is that the kind of joke only two comrades who have lived through battle together can share? Or is she serious? Maybe you'll learn the answer when you get a little more experience.

(If you talk about something else, go to **87**. If you've had enough, return to **the map at 10** and choose a new destination.)

In a corner of the headquarters' central courtyard are two Titans. The Survey Corps managed to capture them during the cleanup of Trost District. The four-meter Titan has been named Sonny, while they're calling the seven-meter one Bean.

You gape. Countless iron nails and thick metal bands have been used to bind them, and some of the elite Survey Corps members are guarding them. But still, it's not pleasant seeing a living Titan before your eyes.

A voice comes from behind you.

"Heh heh heh! Cute, aren't they?"

The person who speaks to you is wearing glasses, their long hair casually tied back. It's Hange Zoë, a squad leader with the Survey Corps. Known as one of the top Titan researchers, Hange is responsible for conducting experiments on these captives.

"Nooow then, I wonder what kind of tests we should do today?"

Hange's face is flushed with what might be happiness. The question doesn't appear to be rhetorical.

What do you say?

"We should see if we can communicate with the Titans." (Go to **34**)

"We should chop those things up." (Go to **52**)

"Tell me about Titans." (Go to **81**)

(If you decide you don't have time for this and leave, return to **the map at 20** and choose a new destination.)

"Ahh! That's a fantastic idea!" Hange exclaims, spreading both arms wide. "If Titans can understand human language, we might be able to learn about them!"

"I thought you already tried that yesterday—and the day before," says the aide next to Hange. "Didn't you conclude that it was impossible to talk to the Titans, or even make ourselves understood?"

"Ah, but Moblit, today could be the day! Let's try a different way of communicating."

With that, Hange approaches the four-meter Titan, Sonny, and waves. Sonny doesn't seem interested. His eyes evince not a shred of intelligence. But he does open his mouth and say, "Ahhhh."

"Hm? What's that? You want to say something, Sonny?" Hange comes even closer.

Suddenly, Sonny clamps his giant mouth shut! His massive teeth make an audible gnashing sound. Hange is only just able to jump back, exclaiming, "Ha ha ha! Did you see that? Sonny responded to my words!"

"He was trying to eat you, Squad Leader!" Moblit objects, dragging Hange back. "If you keep this up, you really are going to die one of these days!"

It looks like this is how these experiments always go… (If you want to spend more time with Hange, go back to **33** and make a different suggestion. If you're tired of playing along, return to **the map at 20** and choose a new destination.)

●35

Annie's eyes soften when you say this.

"Yeah. My father is a worrier. I think it would be better to work on my fighting skills than to use something like this. This wouldn't do any good against a Titan, anyway."

Annie thanks you again. You give her the ring and leave. (Go to **91**)

●36

You pay close attention to Annie's feet, read her movements. She kicks fast and high—but you dodge.

"Well, well." Annie's eyes widen the slightest bit, the hint of a smile passing over her face. "Not bad. Looks like I'd better get serious." A furious flurry of kicks follows.

In the end, Annie works you over; her last strike sends you flying.

Her fighting skills are incredible. You never had a chance of winning.

"You put up a halfway decent fight. Feel free to ask for another lesson sometime."

Annie smiles a little, and walks away in good spirits.

(Increase your **Affinity with Annie** by **1**. Go to **37**)

Annie has been gone for a few minutes before you manage to haul yourself up.

Suddenly you notice something on the ground: a silver-colored metal ring.

Did Annie drop this during the fight? You pick it up.

The ring looks very plain and simple, maybe a bit large for a woman to wear. It looks less like a piece of jewelry and more like maybe it's supposed to protect the finger.

As you fiddle with the ring, you must brush a particular spot by accident, because there's a click and a tiny blade extends. What a nasty little trap. You carefully fold the blade back in.

Now… What do you do with the ring?

Take the underhanded thing back to headquarters (Go to **40**)

Give it back to Annie (Go to **89**)

Leave it (return to **the map at 20**.

If you change your mind, you can come back here and reconsider. Make a note of this section number.)

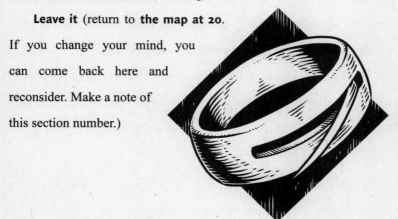

•38

Reiner is well-built and looks like a dependable older brother. In contrast, Bertolt is taller but doesn't look as strong. The vibes they give off are also polar opposites, but they must get along well because they're often together.

You can talk to them. If you ask about which unit they want to join, go to 54. If you ask what they think about Annie, go to 16. If you'd rather go somewhere else, return to **the map at 20**.

•39

You think back to what happened here.

This was several days ago now. Hange came to the old Survey Corps headquarters and began conducting experiments on Eren. The dried-up old well seemed to get Hange's attention. If Eren were to transform while inside it, it would be the perfect size to contain his Titan body so he couldn't move. On the off chance he lost himself and went berserk, it would be possible to observe and even experiment on him. That, at least, was the logic by which Eren was lowered into the well.

During the Battle of Trost, Eren transformed when he felt physical pain. So he kept biting his hand down in that well, until it was covered in blood... but he still didn't transform into a Titan. (Go to 67)

•40

You're just about to head off... when someone attacks you from behind. You're knocked unconscious. (Go to 51)

●41

"Hey, hey. I'm a modest young lady, remember? What do you think you're doing?"

Annie dodges you, moving quickly. In the same motion, she grabs your hand and bends it backward. (Go to **71**)

●42

"Ahh! My dear trainee! So you're interested in the Titans, too?" Hange's face splits into a grin. "And why not? You have a classmate who can turn into one, after all. You know, I'm hoping to get Eren's cooperation in some new experiments on Sonny and Bean. I'm just waiting for permission. Oh—Sonny and Bean are the names of the Titans the Survey Corps captured. They're at Trost District army headquarters right now…" Hange's furiously paced speech suddenly comes to a stop. "Ha ha! I see I've started monologuing. Sorry about that." The smile widens. "I should have started by explaining about our pet Titans and the experiments we've done so far. Let's not just stand here and talk. Let's find somewhere nice to sit down…"

It looks like you're going to be hearing about Titans for the foreseeable future… (Go to **29**)

●**43**

"Huh…" Annie's expression changes. Her usually impassive face betrays just the hint of a happy smile. Or is that the cruel grin of someone who's found their next victim…?

If you're going to back out, now's your chance. Return to **the map at 20** and make a different choice. If, with no thought for your own safety, you forge ahead with the martial arts lesson… go to **44**.

●**44**

You and Annie head for the martial arts practice ground in the courtyard.

"I think it's best to learn from experience," Annie says. "Come at me however you like." Then she assumes a fighting stance.

Her defense is perfect; you see no way through her guard. Take a close look at her and decide what to do.

You…

Fire off your best punch! (Go to **86**)

Grab her in a hug to keep her from moving! (Go to **41**)

Attack quickly, watching out for her kick! (Go to **50**)

•45

You come to an old well. The water has long since dried up.

If this is your first time reading this passage, go to **17.**

If this is not your first time reading this passage, go to **70.**

•46

Her look gets even sharper. "And just what do you mean by that?" she asks.

"What if there was some situation where you had to hurt yourself for some reason?" (Go to **79**)

"I heard some of our comrades shot themselves during the Battle of Trost." (Go to **75**)

•47

You hurry to help Eren. His hand detaches from the massive arm with a popping sound.

"Th-Thanks," he says. The gigantic arm lies on the ground, blowing out steam until it's all but dissolved.

Hange dashes up to the two of you, exclaiming, "No! I wanted to study that!"

(Increase your **Affinity with Eren** by **1** and go to **80**.)

•48

Armin isn't biting. "No," he says, "maybe I misunderstood what I was seeing."

If you keep the secret to yourself, go to **77**.

If you decide to ignore Armin and go after Annie yourself, go to **90**.

•49

Gunther, a member of Squad Levi, passes by, muttering, "The experiments we did here were terrible."

If you ask him what he's talking about, go to **24**.

If you aren't interested, or already know, return to **the map at 10** and choose a new destination.

•50

You think you're being careful, but Annie's kick is astoundingly fast. Her leg lifts higher than you expect. "Hah! Too slow!" Her foot connects with your temple. (Go to **71**)

•51

Not long after, the murder of Sonny and Bean occurs. You are among the corpses that result. They ultimately decide that you killed the Titans out of personal hatred, but that the two fought back and you couldn't escape being killed yourself… (Go to **14**)

"Ooh! I like that!" Hange hefts a steel spear that appears to be intended for use in experiments.

"Didn't you try that the other day?" Hange's aide says.

"The key to a successful experiment is repetition, Moblit! How do Titans respond when injured? Do they feel pain? How quickly can they heal? There are so many things to study!"

With that, the squad leader approaches Bean, the 7-meter Titan, and begins jabbing at him with the spear.

"Waaah!" Bean's wail is uncanny.

"Waaaaaaah!" For some reason, Hange begins wailing, too.

"Why are you making that noise, Squad Leader?" Moblit shouts. "And you're too close—it's dangerous!"

Hange looks back. "How can you not cry back at him? Bean is enduring such pain!" Perhaps it's an excess of emotion that has brought the tears to the squad leader's eyes. "How can you call yourself a researcher if you don't understand the Titans' feelings? Please, Bean, endure! It hurts me, too!" Hange resumes spearing the Titan.

You see the steam of the Titan healing its wounds, and the two wailing voices mingle together… (If you want to continue to entertain Hange, go back to **33** and make another suggestion. If you're tired of this, return to **the map at 20** and choose a new destination.)

Jean Kirstein, a young man who was one of your classmates, is standing and talking with several of the other trainees.

Jean got excellent marks, but his bad attitude during training caused others to resent him. Rumor had it that he was going to pick a cushy life with the Military Police Brigade, as is his right as one of the top scorers.

But something seems to have changed about him since the Battle of Trost. He's started saying that he's decided to join the Survey Corps. He first mentioned it while on cleanup duty after the battle—while bringing in the corpses of his friends and comrades.

It seems like the normal reaction to a firsthand experience of just how terrifying the Titans are would be to want to join the MPs even more. That seems to be what Jean and the soldiers around him are discussing.

"Heh! Just 'cause I want to join the Survey Corps doesn't mean I'm like that suicidal bastard all of a sudden." Jean all but spits the words out. That, at least, hasn't changed.

"'That suicidal bastard'—you mean Eren?" one of your classmates asks. It's a nickname Jean gave Eren when you were all training together. Eren, eager to join the Survey Corps and exterminate the Titans, was often at loggerheads with Jean. Jean would always taunt Eren with this nickname, and it found a certain currency among members of the 104th Training Corps.

And now Jean is planning to join the Survey Corps himself. Life is truly strange. (Go back to **20** and choose a new destination.)

•54

"I'm going to join the Survey Corps," Reiner says. "I know it'll be dangerous, but I want to go back to my hometown, no matter what. I would do anything."

You're impressed, but this is also what you expected from him. Reiner would no doubt help boost the Survey Corps' morale.

In contrast, Bertolt is ambivalent; he seems to want to avoid the entire subject. "I've just been… going with the flow. I really respect the rest of you. You've all got these ideals that you're working toward."

(If you ask what they think of Annie, go to **16**. If you want to go somewhere else, return to **the map at 20**.)

•55

"I'm set on joining the Military Police Brigade," she says. You know that she was ranked fourth among your classmates; the top ten have the option of joining the MPs. "But so what?" she goes on. "Were you going to change your plans based on what I do or something?" Her expression never alters; her eyes are cold.

(If you ask her to teach you martial arts, go to **43**. If you want to go somewhere else, return to **the map at 20**.)

•56

One morning, an urgent dispatch arrives at the old Survey Corps headquarters.

"What?!" Hange exclaims upon hearing the message. "Sonny and Bean—?!" The squad leader rushes off to Trost's army headquarters.

It looks like something big is going on. Captain Levi and the members of the special operations squad hurry around. They decide to take Eren with them (you suspect they can't afford to leave someone behind to guard him). You end up going with them as well.

You all ride to army headquarters as fast as you can. When you arrive, the place is in an uproar. You learn that the two captured Titans have been killed. (Go to **82**)

•57

One morning, you find the army headquarters in an uproar. The two captured Titans were killed in the night.

After a while, Squad Leader Hange arrives, riding as fast as possible. The squad leader was responsible for experimenting on the Titans, but had been somewhere else last night. Bad timing.

"No... And today I was going to get Eren's help to do some new experiments..."

(Go to **82**)

Captain Levi is there. You salute.

You've heard a lot of rumors—that he's the strongest soldier humanity has, that he's a one-man brigade. From up close like this, though, you find him surprisingly small, with few distinguishing features. Yet just standing there, he exudes a sense of intimidation. There's no question this is an experienced soldier.

He's staring right at you. You can't tell if you've done something to earn a glare, or if he just always looks this severe.

"One of Eren's classmates, are you? Did you want something from me?"

You...

Ask about Squad Leader Hange Zoë (Go to 59)

Ask about the Special Operations Squad, aka Squad Levi (Go to **23**)

Ask about Eren (Go to **27**)

•59

"Ah. That Abnormal," he says.

A human Abnormal…? You suppose he just means Hange is strange.

"If the squad leader asks for your help, then help. Even if it ends up being troublesome."

(If you ask him something else, go to **58**. Otherwise, return to **the map at 10** and choose a new destination. The captain is a busy man.)

●**60**

You stand beside Captain Levi, helping him protect Eren.

The members of Squad Levi call out to you:

"What are you doing, trainee? Get away from there!"

"Captain Levi, you have to move, quickly!"

You hear them, but you don't move.

In the meantime, Eren withdraws his own arm from the Titan arm. As the massive appendage begins to waste away, the armed soldiers at last begin to relax. Only Hange is upset, crying, "No! My Titan arm!"

After it's all over, Captain Levi says, "I told you to remain calm. This trainee seems to have a cooler head than anyone else here."

(Increase your **Affinity with Levi** by 1 and go to **80**.)

●**61**

That night, an idea comes to you in a rush. You suddenly remember the discussion of whether Eren needed to bite his hand to transform into a Titan. But if some kind of pain is the key, then there's a better way than biting himself…

You realize there's someone with you, there in the darkness, but a second later you take a sharp blow to the head and lose consciousness. (Go to **51**)

•62

A bearded Survey Corps soldier is there. It's Squad Leader Mike Zacharias, rumored to be the strongest man in the unit after Captain Levi himself.

Suddenly, he brings his face very close to your body and begins sniffing you. Then he snorts—but with a smile—and leaves without saying anything.

What was that all about? You've heard tell that the brutality of the work in the Survey Corps means only the crazies end up here. Maybe he's one of them… (Return to **the map at 20** and choose a new destination.)

•63

You take Eren's other hand and ask him to calm down.

"Hey, that's dangerous!" the soldiers are yelling. "Get away from him, trainee!" But you, instead, call out to Eren.

Maybe it's the presence of a familiar classmate, the fact that he finally has an ally, but Eren starts to grow calmer. Once the soldiers realize he's not going to do any harm, they relax, too.

"Good work! Eren, don't move! Let me see your arm!" Only Hange seems downright excited by this turn of events, and spends the next hour studying and experimenting on the arm until it finally vanishes… (Increase your **Affinity with Hange** by 1 and go to **80**.)

●64

You discover some old graffiti on the wall of the building. It's faded in places, but from what you can make out, it says:

Levi's the best   Survey Corps is the worst   —Ian & Isa—

Maybe it was left by some member of the Survey Corps long ago. It looks like Levi was a valued comrade even then.

(There's no special meaning to this graffiti, but the fact that you found it shows your gift for careful observation, which could lead to you discovering other information in the future. That could be useful. Return to **the map at 10** and choose another destination.)

●65

When you say this, it starts a buzz among your comrades.

"When you put it that way—so would I!"

"I remember Annie and Mikasa being paired up once during training. It was a sight to see!" (Go to **69**)

●66

"The same reason as Eren? What, you think we have matching rings or something?"

Annie shrugs. She doesn't smile. You've never seen Eren with a ring. So why did you think they were related? (Go to **61**)

That isn't the only strange thing to happen that day.

The experiment is called off, and Eren joins Captain Levi and the others at an outdoor table for a break. Without warning, there's a rumbling noise and a cloud of steam. Suddenly Eren, who was seated innocently at the table, has a Titan's arm!

The four members of Squad Levi have their weapons drawn almost instantly and begin flinging questions at Eren.

"Why did you transform into a Titan without permission? Answer me!"

"Move that arm an inch—just an inch—and I'll cut your damn head off!"

Eren himself isn't sanguine about the situation; he groans in distress.

"Shut up and leave me alone for a minute!" he exclaims, but this only agitates the people around him. He begins trying to pull his own arm out of the Titan arm.

Squad Leader Hange is excited: "Let me examine that arm!"

And in the midst of all this confusion…

"Calm down, all of you." Captain Levi alone sounds in control of himself. He inserts himself between Eren and his squad.

With everything going on, what choice do you make?

Help Eren pull his arm out (Go to **47**)

Try to calm Eren down and get him to stop moving (Go to **63**)

Join Levi in trying to stop the Special Operations Squad (Go to **60**)

●68

Mikasa is discussing something with several of her classmates and comrades.

"...That shorty is full of himself. One of these days, I'll take him down a peg..." Mikasa mutters, her face terrifying.

This sets the others chattering. "Shorty? Does she mean Levi…?"

"That's some way to talk about the guy they call humanity's strongest soldier. Mikasa's something else. Looks like she's pretty ticked…"

Mikasa looks at you, her eyes dangerous.

"What do you think?"

How do you answer?

"You mean what happened at the military tribunal? It was necessary." (Go to **30**)

"You'd only put yourself in danger pulling something like that. I wish you wouldn't." (Go to **26**)

"You versus humanity's strongest soldier? Now that I'd like to see." (Go to **65**)

●69

The source of Mikasa's anger is the military tribunal that happened several days ago—Eren's interrogation. Your friends have told you what happened.

There was hostility toward Eren from the start, but when someone testified that after turning into a Titan during the Battle of Trost, Eren had attacked Mikasa, the hostility intensified, becoming a concern that he was a danger to the human race. Mikasa tried to stand up for Eren, but it only led some people to speculate that she herself was a spy for the Titans.

You find this ridiculous. Why would Eren attack Mikasa if she were a Titan spy? The mood in the room was so tense that even such basic lapses of logic were being ignored, which was not going to benefit Eren in the least.

The Military Police Brigade was among the first to suggest that Eren should be executed and an autopsy performed. Eren being Eren, he yelled something like, "Just shut your mouths and invest everything in me!" Which, of course, didn't help matters any.

It was then (you're told) that Captain Levi began kicking Eren mercilessly. Even those who had been calling for execution found a modicum of pity in their hearts at the scene, and so the wrath abated.

Commander Erwin took the opportunity to suggest that Eren be given into the custody of the Survey Corps, and his suggestion was accepted.

No one is sure whether Levi's burst of violence was an act arranged with Eren ahead of time, or a decision he made on the spot. Mikasa looks likely to hold a grudge about it forever—but it was thanks to that brutality that Eren is still alive.

(Return to **the map at 20** and choose a new destination.)

●70

You think back to what happened here. Could this place hold the secret key to Eren's transformations into a Titan?

Forget it. You're no specialist; your thinking about it won't do anyone any good. What's more important is that right now, Eren isn't able to transform of his own volition. (Return to **the map at 10** and choose a new destination.)

●71

Annie proceeds to land a flurry of kicks on you, finishing with a sweep that takes your legs out from under you and sends you sprawling on the ground.

Her fighting technique is astonishing. You had no hope of winning.

"Looks like you're not gonna challenge me anytime soon. Points for effort, though," Annie says with the slightest hint of a smile. "Feel free to ask for another lesson sometime."

(If this is the first time you've read this passage, increase your **Affinity with Annie** by **1**. Otherwise, there's no further effect. If you challenge Annie again, go to **44**. If you've had enough, return to **the map at 20** and choose a new destination.)

●72

That night, you go missing. Later, your body is found somewhere well outside Trost District, still wearing your Vertical Maneuvering Equipment.

The powers that be decide you were the one who murdered Sonny and Bean. Fearing discovery when the investigation began, you fled, but you made a mistake while trying to use your Vertical Maneuvering Equipment at night, and died as a result.

The Military Police Brigade issues its report to this effect, and the case is closed. (Go to **14**)

●73

Squad Leader Hange Zoë is visiting the old Survey Corps headquarters.

Hange is not a member of the Special Operations Squad, but is the premier Titan specialist in the unit. The squad leader seems to be making frequent trips between Trost District army headquarters and this place in order to observe and study Eren.

"Oh! You're one of Eren's fellow trainees!" Hange exclaims upon seeing you, looking happy. Is this how the squad leader always acts…?

"After all you've been through… have you developed an interest in the Titans, too? Anything you want to ask?"

You…

Have something you want to ask (Go to **42**)

Hold back (Return to the map at **10** and choose a new destination)

●74

Your equipment is examined, but it shows no sign of having been used, and you are cleared of suspicion. As are Armin, Connie, and Annie…

Still, something nags at you.

You're released after the conclusion of the investigation. That's when Armin comes up to you.

"You noticed it too, didn't you? The Vertical Maneuvering Equipment Annie presented during the investigation… That wasn't her own gear. That belonged to Marco, who died at Trost." He goes on: "I'm not sure I can believe it myself, but…"

You…

Go after Annie! (Go to 48)

Think Armin must be mistaken (Go to 15)

Keep this revelation secret (Go to 77)

●75

You talk. You tell her how when the army headquarters building was surrounded by Titans and escape seemed impossible, some of your comrades shot themselves to death. They figured it was better than being eaten…

"Yeah," Annie says, "it's a sad story. And I'm just like them. I sure as hell don't want to be eaten by some Titan. If there's ever a time when I have no other choice, I'll use this. Truth is, I'm a coward."

For some reason, she looks almost relieved. You accept it and leave. (Go to 91)

●76

You take Annie at her word. But that night, something occurs to you. When did Annie get so philosophical? For that matter, when did she get her hands on Marco's Vertical Maneuvering Equipment? If she found it on the battlefield, she should have given it back to the unit. It would be very strange if she had secretly kept it, anticipating everything that had just happened…

You realize there's someone behind you in the darkness, but at the same instant, you take a sharp blow to the head and lose consciousness. (Go to **72**)

●77

"I think that's a good idea," Armin nods. "I might just be imagining things… In fact, I hope I am."

You take what you know and store it away in your heart.

You obtain **Key Number A**. It represents the secret you share with Armin. Write the number **77** on your Battle Record Sheet, or commit it to memory. (Increase your **Affinity with Armin** by **1** and go to **95**.)

●78

Armin is discussing something with several of your classmates and comrades. He appears to be talking about the time Eren turned into a Titan. The subject is of great interest, and his audience is rapt. Annie is there, too. She listens without evident interest.

(If you listen, too, go to **9**. Otherwise, return to **the map at 20** and choose a new destination.)

●79

The gleam in Annie's eye grows more and more dangerous.

"What are you talking about? I'm not that type. And when I want to liven things up, I use my fists. This is just... Well, sometimes it's helpful to have a blade around."

This makes sense to you. You give her the ring and leave. (Go to **61**)

●80

Ultimately, the reason for this incident remains mysterious, even to Eren himself.

Hange, after inspection of the bones left behind by the Titan arm, hypothesizes that when he attempted to pick up the spoon, Eren unconsciously turned just a part of himself into a Titan. In other words, pain isn't the only factor; he may be able to transform when he has some sort of goal.

Once they understand what happened, the members of Squad Levi apologize to Eren. You hear that they each bite their own hands hard enough to leave a scar. The soldiers weren't wrong; they were simply loyal to their duty. Eren is quite apologetic himself. (Go to **70**)

●81

"Ahh! My dear trainee! So you're interested in the Titans, too?" Hange's face splits into a grin. "It's true: this isn't the first time we've succeeded in capturing Titans. According to the Survey Corps' records, the first Titans to be taken alive were—" Hange is off and running. You immediately regret saying anything, but you can't stop the squad leader-cum-professor now.

Hange talks at you passionately for the better part of half an hour.

"—and so, this is the first time we've had a chance to observe and experiment on Titans in such a controlled environment. Two of them, no less! Do you understand how fantastic this is?"

You nod. Just as you think the lecture is almost over, Hange's voice rises again.

"On to the main point, then. Thanks to our delightful friends Sonny and Bean, we've managed to learn—"

So all that talk was just preamble.

You spend a very long time that day learning about Titans. (Go to **29**)

All that's left of the **2** Titans is their erstwhile restraints. Those, and something that looks like bones, along with a mark on the ground. Like other Titans, the corpses wasted away immediately after death. The vestiges that remain suggest the Titans died rather than fled.

"Sonny! Bean!" Hange is calling their names and weeping piteously. You would think the squad leader had lost a pair of beloved children.

The area is crawling with soldiers.

"Is it true they were killed?"

"Yeah. This wasn't a natural death. The guard said he heard the sound of Vertical Maneuvering Equipment, but the killer was already gone when he got there."

"Vertical Maneuvering Equipment? So the culprit was with the army?"

"Who else would know how to kill a Titan?"

"Good point. I'll bet this guy had at least a couple of accomplices, too."

"Oh yeah? What makes you say that?"

"You said the killers were already gone when the guard got there, right? No way **1** person could off **2** Titans that fast." (Go to **83**)

●**83**

The scene of the crime is packed with people. Suddenly, you notice Captain Levi and Eren are there, too. Eren takes in his surroundings with a look of shock.

Someone approaches. It's Commander Erwin Smith, the man with ultimate responsibility for the Survey Corps. Is what's going on here so important that the commander himself has come to see it?

You overhear what Erwin says as he walks up to Eren: "What can you see? Who do you think our enemy is?"

You…

Think about what his words might mean (Look at **82**, take any numbers you find there, add them to the number of this section [**83**], and go to that section.)

Don't understand what he's saying, or decide it has nothing to do with you (Go to **93**)

(Hint: *if you look carefully*, it all adds up.)

●**84**

Your equipment is investigated, but (naturally) it shows no sign of having been used, and you are cleared of doubt.

The Vertical Maneuvering Equipment of your other comrades, Armin, Annie, and Connie, is similarly clean. Apparently the killer isn't among you. (Go to **95**)

There's Krista. She's with Ymir, the freckled girl who's often by her side. Krista is a sweet young woman who shows kindness to everyone, making her very popular. Ymir, on the other hand, is sharp-tongued and ruthless. The two of them couldn't be more different, yet they've been close since basic. They're talking about something. It sounds like they're discussing their futures, which they'll have to decide soon.

"I… I think I'll join the Survey Corps," Krista says. "To help everyone." She's one of the top scorers in your class and could join the Military Police Brigade, but maybe her experiences in Trost have changed her mind.

"You sure? You're shaking awful hard as you say that," Ymir says with a shrug. "If you're just doing it for others' sake, then don't."

Ymir can be rather rough, but she seems concerned about Krista. She notices you watching them. "What are you looking at?" she asks.

(Return to **the map at 20** and choose a new destination.)

●86

Annie dodges quickly, then throws you.

"When you just try to fire off your strongest punch, your movements get broader. You leave yourself open." (Go to **71**)

●87

"Captain Levi is amazing," Petra says. "He personally selected us—it's an honor."

The other three nod. You can tell how much they trust and respect Captain Levi. He impresses even these experienced soldiers.

"I'm going to give everything I've got to completing this mission," Gunther says.

"Me, too," adds Eld.

The "mission" in question is protecting Eren. But when you say as much, the others act strangely uneasy.

"R-Right," says Petra. "We're going to look after your friend, of course we are."

"Yeah," says Eld. "I mean... Eren's got it rough, too."

From the way they're talking, you realize that yes, they are protecting Eren, but at the same time they're keeping watch on him so that they can respond if and when necessary. You see that each of the four soldiers has bite marks on their hand. There's a lot going on with Eren.

Finally, the talk turns to Squad Leader Hange Zoë. Everyone seems to share a tacit understanding about this person.

"The squad leader is very... passionate about Titan research."

"Just... try to avoid telling Hange that you want to learn about Titans or anything. Trust us."

Such is their advice to you.

(If, now that you think about it, you're bothered by the way Oluo spoke to you, go to **32**. If you don't mind, return to **the map at 10** and choose a new destination.)

You take in the scene and think over what you've heard.

The two Titans have been killed; that much is obvious. Whether or not there were two or more killers isn't certain. The murder of both Titans in such a short period of time suggests the possibility, but it could also be the work of a single, extraordinarily talented individual. The fact that both Titans were killed probably means something. For example, maybe someone wanted to stop the Survey Corps from experimenting any further... If it was done out of sympathy, they could have just killed one of them and then beat feet.

"It looks like you've worked something out."

The voice startles you. Commander Erwin is talking to you.

You hurriedly tell him what you've been thinking. Maybe it will help somehow.

"Hmm," the commander says, an odd expression on his face. It doesn't seem like you've given him the answer he was looking for. But he says, "So you considered what was going on here and figured the numbers had significance. Not a bad thought. I hope you'll remember the lesson. What's your name?"

You tell him, and he nods.

"I'll remember it."

You might not have given him the answer he expected, but you've proven yourself worthy of a spot in his memory. Suddenly, you realize Captain Levi is looking at you. He's as expressionless as ever, but he seems to have heard everything.

(You seem to have gotten Levi's attention as well. Increase your **Affinity with Levi** by 1 and go to **94**.)

●89

You take the ring back to Annie. "Thanks," she says, but there's a hard edge to the look she gives you. She accepts the ring and glances at you. She seems to have figured out that you know its little secret.

"Why do you think I carry this?"

What do you say?

"For protection?" (Go to **35**)

"To use it on yourself?" (Go to **46**)

"For the same reason Eren does?" (Go to **66**)

●90

You follow Annie to a deserted corner. She looks down and says softly, "I wanted to take revenge for my comrades. Marco was killed by the Titans, so I used his Vertical Maneuvering Equipment to get back at them. Any chance you could keep it to yourself? I'll turn myself in to headquarters when the time is right." (Go to **76**)

●91

You obtain **Key Number R, the secret of the ring**. Write down or remember the number **40**. If you're done, return to **the map at 20** and choose a new destination.

It is decided that all military personnel in the building will submit their Vertical Maneuvering Equipment to be inspected for signs of use. You trainees are among those gathered in the main hall. You set your equipment on a table, and one by one the units are inspected. As you stand at attention waiting for your turns, some of your comrades begin to whisper to each other.

"Who knew they'd punish you for killing a Titan?"

"No way there's a criminal among us… I'm totally wiped from cleaning up the battlefield all day…"

You just stand there, listening. Armin, Connie, and Annie are all standing nearby. They, too, are conversing quietly. Connie seems to be worried about which unit he should join, and he's talking to Armin and Annie about it. Come to think of it, both Connie and Annie scored well enough that they could join the Military Police Brigade.

"Maybe I should join the Survey Corps," he mutters, but immediately says, "Hey, Annie… You think the Military Police Brigade would be better?"

"If somebody told you to die, would you?" Annie says bluntly. "Then you should do what you want to do."

"Annie, you're actually pretty nice," says Armin. "It seems like you don't want us to join the Survey Corps… and I bet you have a reason for joining the Military Police." He keeps his eyes fixed on the table as he speaks.

"I just… want to save myself," Annie mutters.

Can you take their conversation at face value? Or is there some deeper meaning…? (Go to **84**)

●93

"Come again?" Eren looks perplexed. It seems he didn't understand what Commander Erwin said. It makes no sense to you, either. Captain Levi is standing nearby—did he understand?

"Sorry," Erwin says after a moment. "I didn't mean to ask such a strange question."

Then he disappears into the crowd. (Go to **94**)

●94

You're curious about what Commander Erwin meant, but you don't have time to think about it because Trost District army headquarters is soon in an uproar.

The culprit is believed to be a soldier, so everyone who has been in or out of headquarters recently is a suspect. That includes the 104th Training Corps—and you. It doesn't matter if you were somewhere else that night. You might have lent some equipment to one of the conspirators.

Eren, who has been under lock and key and without his equipment in another location entirely, is the only one who doesn't seem to be under suspicion... (Go to **92**)

●95

The inspection ends. It seems no one's Vertical Maneuvering Equipment shows signs of having been used.

Some say, "I knew it had to be an outside job. No way any of us is a criminal." But there are others who whisper that the killer must have had some clever way of deceiving the inspectors.

Days pass, and the criminal isn't found. You and the others finish your assigned duty of cleaning up from the Battle of Trost. The Survey Corps, which had borrowed this facility in order to experiment on the Titans, gives it back to its rightful owners, the Trost Guard Unit of the Garrison, and withdraws. With their "subjects" murdered, there's no more reason for them to be here.

As for you and the other the members of the 104th Training Corps, you continue working your way through the red tape required to become full soldiers. The day when you decide what path you'll take—which was supposed to be the very day that became the Battle of Trost—finally arrives.

You hear that Commander Erwin of the Survey Corps, which is currently sharing the headquarters building with you, will be giving a speech to solicit new members. At the commander's request, all members of the 104th Training Corps are required to attend, but which path you take remains your free choice.

More than a few of your comrades want to join the Survey Corps, and plenty more saw the unit in action during the Battle of Trost. Nobody objects to hearing what Commander Erwin has to say.

You line up in front of a stage with the rest of your classmates and listen. (Go to **96**)

"I'm Commander Erwin Smith of the Survey Corps. You're standing in the spot where my unit received its commission from the king."

This is all the preamble he offers; he moves immediately into his main subject.

"In the recent Titan attack, everyone here experienced what the average excursion outside is like. As a result, I'm sure you've come to know your own limits, and the terror of the Titans. However." His voice rises. "Despite all the people we lost in that attack, humanity was able to seize a victory such as we have never known. And Eren Yeager holds the key."

Erwin goes on to talk about Eren's achievements, and to suggest that he may be able to make clear the true nature of the Titans. He also tells you that the secret of the Titans is hidden in the basement of Eren's birth home.

"If we can retake Wall Maria and just get to that basement, we may be able to escape from these 100 years of domination by the Titans."

This starts everyone chattering. You've never heard anything like this before.

"But," Commander Erwin goes on, "it will be necessary to retake Wall Maria for this to work. With the gate of Trost District no longer usable, we'll need to find an alternate route. Over the past 4 fruitless years, casualties in the Survey Corps have been very high,

with 9 out of 10 dead. Conservatively, to send a major unit to Wall Maria would require 5 times that long."

Everyone starts talking again.

"The Survey Corps is perennially short on personnel. We need new members. I won't try to hide it: if you join our unit, you will be asked to participate in our expedition beyond the walls 1 month from now. 5 in 10 new recruits die on their first expedition. Those who survive, however, become exceptional soldiers with a high survival rate."

Finally, the commander says, "That's all I have to say. Most of those who join the Survey Corps will die. If, knowing that, you still want to be part of our unit, then please remain here."

Which unit do you join?

The Survey Corps (Go to **97**)

The Garrison (Go to **140**)

The Military Police Brigade (Go to **163**)

Alternatively, if you think there's a deeper meaning to what Commander Erwin said, **look around carefully and consider your options.**

After everything Commander Erwin has said, most of the unit leaves. Many of them had already decided to join some other branch of service. You see Annie among them. She must have settled on the Military Police Brigade.

You're sure there were more people than this who wanted to join the Survey Corps... But the commander's vivid and upsetting speech seems to have scared them off. Then again, there are those who have chosen to remain, speech or no speech. Some are trying not to let their teeth chatter, while others appear to be crying. You are among those who stay.

Commander Erwin looks down from his platform at the few who remain.

"If you were told to die, could you do it?" he asks you.

"I don't wanna die!" somebody wails.

"I see..." The commander nods, apparently satisfied. "I like the look of each of you. I welcome you as new members of the Survey Corps!"

He salutes you, placing his right hand on his chest—symbolizing how soldiers offer up their very hearts. You all salute him in return.

"You have withstood your fear well... You're all brave soldiers.."

Including yourself, 21 people remain to become members of the Survey Corps. You're provided with new uniforms. You remove your familiar trainee outfit and replace it with one bearing the "Wings of Freedom."

You and your comrades are now members of the Survey Corps. (Go to **98**)

I SEE 21 MEMBERS IN THE 104TH SURVEY CORPS WHO HAVE GIVEN THE SALUTE.

YOU HAVE MY HEARTFELT RESPECT.

YOU HAVE WITHSTOOD YOUR FEAR WELL... YOU'RE ALL BRAVE SOLDIERS.

ONE MONTH LATER

And so, after a month of training...

The day finally comes for the Survey Corps to make its next expedition beyond the walls, with its newly minted members from the 104th Training Corps in tow.

Karanes District is to be your staging area. It's furthest to the east, one of the cities established at the four cardinal compass points along Wall Rose.

The place looks a lot like Trost District. A huge gate, topped by fixed gun emplacements, separates what's behind the wall from what's beyond it. The guns occasionally fire in the direction of whatever is out there. They're clearing away Titans in the area around the gate so the expedition can leave.

Those of you comprising the expedition are already lined up at the gate, all of you waiting on horseback, the cannon fire ringing overhead.

You've never been on an expedition outside the walls before, but this seems like an awfully large group.

You remember Commander Erwin explaining earlier: "One of our objectives on this mission is to get all of our new recruits, Eren Yeager included, some real-life battle experience. For that reason, we plan a relatively brief expedition this time. Additional goals include some exploratory scouting and a delivery to our resource dump. This will further the Survey Corps' long-standing mission to secure a route into Wall Maria."

You take another look at the group participating in this expedition. You still think it looks like a lot of people for a short trip. The baggage train alone is considerable. No doubt much of it is intended for the resource dump.

Although the commander didn't mention it, you suspect part of this expedition is about making sure Eren has some success in battle. If Eren, the human soldier who can transform into a Titan, were able to achieve great things outside the walls, it would prove that he carried the hope of humanity—and that would silence the Military Police Brigade and his other critics.

But for now, it's the cannons that go quiet. A voice comes from beyond the wall, the signal that everything is ready.

"Open the gate!"

With a tremendous creaking and shuddering, the gate of Karanes District slowly begins to open.

"It's almost time! We're going to take another step forward for humanity!" The Survey Corps leaders shout to you. "Show us the fruits of your training!"

You and all your fellow participants in this expedition have been waiting in formation on horseback just inside the gate. Now you raise a great noise.

"The 57th expedition beyond the walls shall now begin! All troops, move out!"

The moment the gate opens wide enough to permit passage, the entire unit surges forth as one. (Go to 99)

Outside the gate, you find the old city spread out before you. Humans used to live here—until five years ago, when the Titans destroyed Wall Maria.

Now it's a ghost town beset by wandering Titans. The expeditionary force moves through it in a pack. There's a great clatter of hooves as dozens of horses ride through the empty streets.

Suddenly, a Titan appears from the shadow of a building.

"Left-front! Ten-meter approaching!"

The preemptive cannon barrages never clear away all the Titans, and anyway, where humans gather, so will Titans.

Soldiers with Vertical Maneuvering Equipment respond. They came down into the city ahead of the rest of you to help keep the expedition safe and support you as extra muscle. Instantaneously, a life-and-death struggle between humans and Titans breaks out in the city.

Voices fly back and forth:

"Protect the column with your lives!"

"Stay calm! Let the support unit do its job—keep marching!"

With people and horses and baggage carts packed so close together, a wayward strike from a Titan could be disastrous. Getting through the city as fast as possible is your first test.

You draw on everything that was pounded into you over a month of training.

"Forward!"

"Keep going!"

You run as hard as you can—and then you're out of the city. Ahead of you lies wasteland.

Someone shouts an order: "Form up in long-distance enemy-scouting formation!"

The expeditionary unit, which had been marching in single file, breaks up into predetermined squads and spreads out across the vast area.

Long-distance enemy-scouting formation is an arrangement supposedly promulgated by Commander Erwin, and it takes up a great deal of space. The various squadrons, marching at specified intervals, communicate via colored smoke signal and messengers on horseback, in order to quickly alert the rest of the formation if they encounter a Titan.

Wherever an enemy appears, a swift response is possible, allowing the unit as a whole to evade danger. The adoption of this formation precipitated a dramatic jump in the survival rate among the Survey Corps.

You new recruits spent the last month in intensive training in order to be a part of this.

"Listen up, recruit," one of the more experienced soldiers once told you. "The Survey Corps is in the business of figuring out how not to fight Titans."

You once believed that the Survey Corps were elite soldiers who went toe-to-toe with the Titans—but it turns out to be the opposite. The most important thing on an expedition beyond the walls are your duties to secure a route and do reconnaissance, and then to avoid contact with Titans, doing the minimum amount of combat necessary to protect your comrades if you do encounter one. The experienced members of the ranks drill this into you.

You learn that the reason the casualty rate in this unit is so high is that sometimes the Titans are simply too big. Those who survive to become experts at fighting the Titans do so precisely because of this commitment to the minimum amount of combat—and nothing more. (Turn the page and look at **the strategic map at 100**, then choose your position.)

100 **57th EXPEDITION BEYOND THE WALLS STRATEGIC MAP**

RIGHT WING FRONT (GO TO 202)
- ARMIN
- NESS & SISS

CENTER FRONT (GO TO 101)
- COMMANDER ERWIN
- HANGE

LEFT WING CENTER COLUMN (GO TO 122)
- SASHA
- MIKASA
- CONNIE

Where were you stationed, again? Choose your location and go to that passage.

STOHESS DISTRICT

KARANES DISTRICT

THE CAPITAL

WALL SHEENA

EHRMICH DISTRICT

WALL ROSE

THE TITAN FOREST

TROST DISTRICT

WALL MARIA

SHIGANSHINA DISTRICT (RUINS)

RIGHT WING REAR (GO TO 149)
- JEAN
- REINER

CENTER REAR (GO TO 105)
- EREN
- LEVI
- SQUAD LEVI

TAIL (GO TO 233)
- KRISTA
- YMIR
- BERTOLT

●101

You show up at the center front, but there's no way you belong here. As you might have noticed when you looked at the strategic plan, not a single one of your fellow rookies is stationed here. Even among the members of the Survey Corps, only the longest-standing—and longest-lived—are present. (Return to **100** and choose a different destination.)

●102

Running becomes your entire world. Finally, you burst through the trees and into an open area.

You look around. You see Jean, on horseback. There are no more Titans nearby. You and the others approach the horse.

"Did you see how the old guard looked back there?" Jean asks. "I don't think even the Survey Corps has ever seen a group of Titans like that before."

You nod. You may be outside the walls, but an attack by such a large number of Titans at once seems unusual.

"Heeeey! Are you okay?" a friend calls, riding up. It's Reiner. Looks like he's all right. "My squad was attacked by a horde of Titans, too," he says. "We had to scatter to get away."

It looks like the right wing is in more than a little trouble right now. And you thought this formation was supposed to be exceptionally safe… (Go to **107**)

●103

One of the more experienced soldiers volunteers to carry out instructions. You approach Sasha hesitantly. She looks like she's going to die.

"I'm so hungry…"

You…

Feel silly for worrying, and leave her alone. (Go to **137**)

Give her something to eat. (Go to **294**)

●104

A little while later… You hear another strange voice, this time from within the forest. It's like a scream mixed with an animal cry. You've never heard anything like it. Is it the voice of a Titan? Krista trembles, terrified.

Suddenly, the Titans lose all interest in you; as one, they make for the woods.

"What in the world…?" Krista's teeth are chattering. She looks like she might fall out of the tree. Despite her obvious fear, though, she tries to put on a brave front, saying, "Something terrible must have happened in there. We have to go help them."

You…

Hold Krista close, to protect her. (Go to **272**)

Say that you'll go into the woods yourself. (Go to **136**)

●105

You are assigned to the same unit as Eren. Captain Levi and the Special Operations Squad are protecting him. This unit is in the center and towards the rear of the formation—by far the most protected spot.

Eren's presence here is a surprise to you. He's an important person, and his location hasn't been divulged to the entire expedition.

You ride up alongside Eren and Captain Levi. For a time, things are startlingly peaceful. The danger you all faced before assuming this formation seems like a distant memory.

Levi and the others are silent. The only sound is the clopping of horses' hooves.

Once in a while, a smoke signal goes up in the distance, or messengers come and go, but on the whole everything is so calm that you would never imagine you were in the Titan-infested lands outside the walls.

Then again, maybe it's precisely because this is the safest part of the formation… (Go to **259**)

●106

"If you're worried about Eren… I'm sure he'll be fine," you say.

"I know," Mikasa says, her voice still calm. Her expression doesn't change.

(Increase your **Affinity with Mikasa** by **1** and go to **274**.)

"Hey, there's a horse," Reiner says.

The animal is carrying Survey Corps equipment, but it has no rider. Reiner runs up close and grabs the reins. "It must have thrown off whoever was riding it," he says. "They might still be nearby—and alive."

You work your way around the area, looking closely. Some distance away, you spot someone sitting on the ground.

It's Armin.

"You okay? Can you stand up, Armin?" Reiner asks, leading the horse over.

Happily, Armin appears to be unharmed. He gets back on his horse.

You've all linked back up. You ride side by side, talking. Armin seems to be alone. What happened to the rest of his unit?

"I'm... I'm the only survivor," he says with a shake of his head. "Ness and all our other senior hands were killed... by that."

You look. Up ahead, you see the back of a Titan who is running along. It has a slim, feminine body... A female Titan.

(**Mark Dieter Ness and Luke Siss dead,** increase the **Kill Count** by **1**, and go to **148**.)

Bertolt and Ymir are assigned to the same place as you.

Bertolt seems fidgety, as always. "Bertolt," Ymir is saying, "you don't happen to know where my Krista is, do you?"

You continue trying to draw off the Titans. Maybe they have some capacity to learn, because they slowly begin to climb the trees.

Bertolt had been worried, but it doesn't look like his abilities with the Vertical Maneuvering Equipment have rusted at all. Ymir, for her part, dodges the Titans flawlessly, looking almost bored.

You yourself somehow manage to avoid the Titans—and the mission continues.

•109

You charge at the Female Titan's head. You see her eye open wide in anger.

That's impossible. She couldn't have healed yet—

But even as you think this, you find yourself caught by the Titan's gaping mouth, and you are devoured. Your last thought before consciousness leaves you is:

I hope my sacrifice contributes to our victory... (Go to **14**)

•110

Thanks to the exceptional reconnaissance system this formation represents, you're able to advance while avoiding any Titans. Once in a while you see a smoke signal go up. Your own squad leader sends up a signal in response, and sometimes you all change direction.

Suddenly, you see a Titan approaching at a terrific speed. Ten-meter class; an Abnormal.

"We've got no choice but to engage the Abnormal!" Squad Leader Ness exclaims. "Siss, you take the nape! I'll keep it pinned!"

Working together, Siss and Squad Leader Ness bring their horses up on either side of the Titan. The creature is running strangely, pitched slightly backward. It's a little more oval-shaped than a human.

Squad Leader Ness sets his anchors in the Titan from horseback, then goes into a leap, cutting into its leg. As the Titan loses its balance and starts to fall forward, Siss jumps onto its back, cutting into the nape of its neck to destroy it.

It's a perfect tandem attack. Using Vertical Maneuvering Equipment out here on the flat plains, with no buildings to assist, is supposed to be difficult, and yet—well, that's two experienced Titan fighters for you. (Go to **121**)

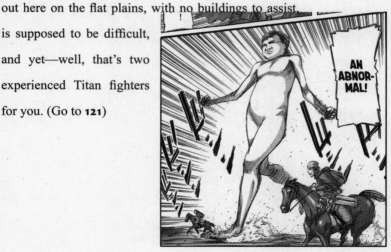

AN ABNOR-MAL!

Suddenly, a Titan appears from the shadow of the abandoned building.

"Oh no, there's one now!" Sasha cries.

The Titan must be ten meters tall. It comes at you on all fours, crawling at a stunning speed. The movement is like some sort of insect. Sasha screams and starts fleeing.

"The scouts must have missed this enemy!" one of the experienced soldiers yells. "This is not good. Draw it this way!"

You…

Rush to help Sasha! (Go to **147**)

Help the other soldiers (Go to **301**)

Both of them look back at you.

"And just how is that?!" they yell in unison, staring daggers at you.

…They're even more alike than you thought. (Go to **184**)

●113

You try to explain, but it's hard to have a complicated conversation while flying with vertical maneuvering. Not to mention, you find it difficult to explain in simple terms the unbelievable things you just witnessed.

"Failed? Under those circumstances? But how?"

"What do you mean, a horde of Titans showed up?"

Nobody quite seems to accept what you're saying.

You're slow, but thankful, to notice the figure coming toward you. It's wearing a Survey Corps cape. The hood is pulled up, so you can't see its face, but it has to be... (Go to **176**)

●114

"Oh, him? I'm sure they've got him in the safest place they can find around here. He's Mr. Titan after all, oh so important." Ymir says. There's a bitter edge to her voice.

"You don't have to talk like that," Krista says. "I think it must be terrible for Eren, carrying that burden."

"He has a strong will of his own," Bertolt says. "Someone like me just gets ignored by everyone." He looks at the ground. (Go to **194**)

You send up a smoke signal and wait for a nearby unit to send help.

At last, you see someone approaching with extra horses. It's Krista, a girl from your training squadron. "Are you okay? I found some lost horses... And then I saw your smoke signal."

You're saved, thanks to Krista. Squad Leader Ness, along with Siss, both cheer.

"We're saved!"

"This girl is like a goddess!"

Krista has brought Ness's horse, along with the others that fled. You're all on horseback again.

All around you, you see smoke signaling the presence of Titans go up.

"We're going to go reinforce the units that are being attacked," Ness and Siss say to you and Armin. "You new kids, head for the center of the formation and tell them about the Female Titan."

"I'm going back to my assigned unit," Krista says. "Ymir will be worried." Then she leaves. (Go to **227**)

●116

A wire drags Gunther into the air, where he's shaken like a ragdoll. Blood comes flying out of him. His neck breaks, his head hanging at an unnatural angle.

(**Mark Gunther Schultz dead**, increase the **Kill Count** by **1**, and go to **156**.)

●117

You head off for the neighboring squadron with your message and inform the squad leader about the events with the crawling Titan.

"Understood. Link up with my squadron; we'll work together!" he says.

Mikasa and Connie are in this unit.

"How's it going with your squad?" Connie calls out. You tell them briefly about what happened.

Then, you...

Ask them about Sasha (Go to **225**)

Ask them about Eren (Go to **212**)

●118

Jean is there, cheering. Armin and Reiner are with him.

"You saved our necks," Jean says. "Armin's horse got done in. We were just talking about which of us would have to stay behind."

"Thank goodness we made it," Krista says, tears in her eyes.

You, too, are glad to see her rewarded this way.

Jean, Armin, and Reiner look at Krista as though beholding a goddess.

You wouldn't mind reminding them that you helped in this rescue, too... But, well, she really is divine. (Go to **157**)

●119

You jump at her as well, attempting to restrain her.

Do you know Key Number R? If so, add it to the number of this passage and go to that passage. If not, go to 142.

●120

You're the only hope!

Determined, you slice at the Female Titan. You don't have to be victorious. You just have to buy some time.

Even while trying to climb the wall, the Female Titan is a powerful opponent. She lashes out with one hand, attacking despite her unstable position. You try to strike at her eye; she opens her mouth and attempts to eat you.

You respond with vertical maneuvering, but she grabs your wire and slams you against the wall.

You feel consciousness growing faint. But just at that moment, you spot other soldiers launching themselves at the Female Titan. Your comrades haven't wasted the precious time you gained them.

Under the assault of several soldiers using vertical maneuvering, the Female Titan finally falls.

(Your actions were admirable. Increase your **Affinity with any one character** by 1 and go to **322**.)

Another new Titan appears in the distance. You can hear its footsteps pounding as it dashes toward you. Another Abnormal? The Titan bends forward as it runs, its form excellent. It looks like it's over ten meters.

"Another one?" Ness says. "Siss, here we go again." Then he turns to you and Armin. "You, rookies, go on ahead. Send up a smoke signal."

You don't like the way this feels. The Titan running at you isn't ovoid, but very much humanoid. That in itself is strange for a Titan. Its body looks like that of a slim young woman.

You...

Do as Ness tells you (Go to **252**)

Will fight the Titan, too! (Go to **315**)

Urge Ness not to fight (Go to **200**)

You are assigned to the same unit as Sasha. According to the strategic map, Mikasa and Connie are around here, too.

Mikasa received excellent marks in training. During the Battle of Trost, she comported herself in a way well beyond that of a mere trainee.

Sasha also had strong grades. Her constant hunger is the most noticeable thing about her, but she also seems to have an almost animalistic intuition; she might be surprisingly capable in battle. You recall that in just the last month of training, she's become quite proficient at horseback riding.

(Increase your **Affinity with Sasha** by 1 and go to **235**.)

●123

Bertolt grows paler and paler.

Out of concern, you decide to stay here. Krista and Ymir go to bring support.

As Ymir leaves, she says to you, "Keep a close eye on Bertolt there. And you, Bertolt, don't do anything funny. Think about just letting this one go."

Then they ride away. (Go to **204**)

●124

Deep in the forest, the command squadron and the baggage train come to a halt.

Another squadron that went on ahead is already there; they've made preparations of some kind.

One of the wagons, which was supposedly carrying supplies, is lying on its side. It turns out it was carrying neither food nor resources. It was piled with barrels—and those barrels are fixed to the wagon. Now on its side, they look like an assembly of small cannons. Maybe this wagon was actually built for an eventuality like this. You've never seen such a thing before.

"This weapon serves to bind a specific target," Hange mutters beside you. "I can't say more than that. Explanations come later."

All you can do is look, but every indication is that this equipment and the activity surrounding it have been under preparation for some time.

Commander Erwin has overseen all of this; he's been readying a secret plan. (Go to **220**)

●**125**

You all get out of the woods, somehow managing to secure horses and join up with the main unit.

When you get out of the Titan Forest, you find Commander Erwin along with the rest of the main unit and all your friends.

Eren is covered in some viscous liquid and is unconscious, but safe. (Go to **130**)

Cautiously, you approach the Female Titan on horseback.

Suddenly, however, the Titan spins on her heel and starts running at a tremendous speed. She closes in on Armin, then kicks his horse and sends it flying!

In the same motion she kneels down, bringing her face close to where Armin lies in the dirt.

"Armin!" From the back of his own horse, Jean fires his anchors at the Titan, transitioning immediately into vertical maneuvering. In a superb display, he gets close to the Titan's back. He should be able to finish it off—at least, he could if it were a normal Titan.

The Female Titan covers the nape of her neck with her hand. She knows her own weak point.

She'll grab the wire and smash Jean to pieces!

At that moment, someone starts shouting. "Jean! Take revenge!" It's Armin, who has stood up. "Take revenge for that suicidal bastard! She stomped him to death!"

You don't understand what he's talking about. Has Armin gone insane?

The Female Titan, however, stopped moving immediately. Almost as if she were reacting to Armin's words...

Jean takes the opening to drop to the ground. Then, another human form comes flying from the Titan's foot. It's Reiner!

He tries to take advantage of the Titan's distraction to attack the nape—but the Titan glares at him and grabs him out of the air. Reiner is clasped in a huge hand… There's a puffing sound and a crimson liquid goes flying everywhere.

"What?!" Jean bellows. "Reinerrrr!"

But then, something comes spinning out of the Titan's hand. It's Reiner. He has drawn his sword and cut off the Titan's fingers; he jumps down and lands on the ground. The red liquid was the Titan's blood.

You swallow. Reiner is an incredible soldier. (Go to **191**)

●127

The Female Titan crouches down, reaching into the underground tunnel; she stands up again and stamps on the ground. She seems to be attacking Eren and the others. (Increase the **Kill Count** by 3.)

They'll be in trouble at this rate.

Check your Battle Record Sheet. Include Marco Bott in your count.

If 5 or more people are dead, go to 308.

If 4 or fewer people are dead, go to 169.

●128

"We should tell a nearby squad about this abandoned village, and the Titan," the squad leader says. "Any volunteers to take a message?"

The communication is to be carried to the squad where Mikasa and Connie are. Sasha is pale, perhaps on account of the battle with the Titan.

You…

Stay close; you're worried about Sasha (Go to 103)

Take the message to where Mikasa is (Go to 117)

●129

You've been riding for a while when you encounter Jean and Reiner, sharing a horse.

"Thank goodness!" Reiner says. "This horse wasn't going to put up with two riders much longer."

They tell you how they encountered a new type of Titan, and fought it together with Armin. Where is Armin?

"He's…" Jean trails off, his eyes downcast. "Damn it. If only this extra horse could have come sooner… I never thought he was good for much, but… he did himself proud. He told us he would stay behind. Told us to report to Commander Erwin instead."

(Mark Armin Arlert dead.)

You're shocked. But what is this important information that Armin left as his last will and testament? Jean is about to tell you, but Reiner cuts him off.

"This is crucial stuff. We'd better not talk about it to just anybody. We should hurry to find the commander. Armin would have wanted that."

"Yeah… You're right, Reiner."

The two of them take the horse from you and ride off. (Go to **161**)

The formation is reformed on the western edge of the woods, but at a significantly smaller scale than when you set out. Losses have been serious. What percentage of the expedition's soldiers is still alive? Most of the baggage train was destroyed in the Titan Forest. You don't know whether the point of this expedition beyond the walls was really to bolster a supply dump, as you were told, or if there was something else going on—but you understand that it has all come to nothing.

Those who are too badly hurt to move are loaded onto the handful of remaining baggage carts. The unconscious Eren is among them.

Even Captain Levi is wounded, his foot injured fighting the Female Titan as he tried to save Eren. He looks okay riding his horse, but you've heard he won't be able to use vertical maneuvering for a while...

"This is a general retreat," Commander Erwin says. "Everyone, back to Karanes District!"

The commander's expression doesn't change as he forcefully issues the order. But how must he feel in his heart? Massive losses, empty hands, and Eren wasn't even able to achieve his Titan form.

This time, you lost. (Go to 247)

Levi listens to him, absolutely silent. He seems to be staring at nothing; his expression never flinches.

You can't stand it anymore, and find somewhere else to be. (Go to **248**)

The first thing you have to do is calm down and tend to Armin's wounds. His Vertical Maneuvering Equipment is, thankfully, undamaged.

The danger of the Female Titan seems to have passed, but you have another problem: you don't have enough horses.

Armin's mount is no good, and Jean's horse has run away. Jean has been whistling for his horse for some time now, but there's no sign of the animal.

Your own horse is injured, and won't be able to support two people.

Reiner's horse might be able to take two riders… but that would mean leaving one person behind.

Who do you think should have to stay behind?

Reiner (Go to **267**)

Jean (Go to **239**)

Armin (Go to **260**)

You yourself (Go to **287**)

Try to somehow get all four of you on horseback (Go to **183**)

●133

You ride on. Your position at the very back affords you a modicum of peace.

Sometimes you see a smoke signal in the distance, and the formation changes direction. This goes on and on.

Are those soldiers up ahead, the men and women under those smoke signals, encountering danger? You hear Krista murmur, "I hope all our friends are all right…"

What do you talk about with the people around you?

Bring up Armin (Go to **255**)

Bring up Eren (Go to **114**)

Bring up Annie, who's now with the Military Police Brigade (Go to **166**)

●134

The soldiers around you all wear dark expressions. The fatigue accounts for some of this, but mostly you suspect it's because the plan has failed.

Hange is there, too. "There goes my big chance… Damn it!" the researcher groans.

Commander Erwin looks unperturbed as he dispenses orders to the squad leaders. Even Captain Levi has his orders—to make sure extra gas and spare blades are available. The unit is preparing to fight tooth and nail, and Levi's strength will be important.

If you accompany Levi, go to **173**.

If you stay with the commander and Hange, go to **302**.

●135

"We're moving forward!" Eren shouts.

A palpable relief passes through the members of Squad Levi. Nobody feels lost now. They ride ahead at full tilt.

From behind come the screams of soldiers, rising up and then being cut off.

(If the Kill Count is 1 or greater, increase it by 2 now. If it is 0, do not change it.)

You glance to the side and see distress written on Eren's face. He's made his choice, but it was a difficult one.

You advance as the soldiers trying to slow down the Female Titan sacrifice themselves behind you, yet slowly but surely, the Female Titan makes up ground. Then she's within arm's reach.

A massive hand reaches out. It's about to grab Eren... (Go to **221**)

●136

No sooner have you said this than another voice breaks in.

"Hey, Krista, are you all right?"

It's Ymir, a girl Krista is friends with. She seems to have come from somewhere else. Her ability to intuit where Krista is must be a sort of instinct. (Go to **182**)

●137

For a while, things are peaceful. But then…

A messenger arrives and tells you that something strange has happened to the right wing, over on the other side of the formation. Some kind of enemy attack. You further learn that the right wing has taken a devastating blow. Even the experienced soldiers are taken aback.

This is the opposite of what Sasha predicted. It seems she was wrong after all…

(**Mark Dieter Ness and Luke Siss dead**, and increase the **Kill Count** by **5**.)

You start to worry about your friends on the right flank.

A smoke signal goes up from the front. The entire formation is being ordered to make a major change in direction, perhaps to deal with the new situation. Your squad wheels around as well. (Go to **150**)

●138

You throw yourself off the wall, hoping to distract the Female Titan.

You don't know if it works, but at least it doesn't seem to hurt.

Mikasa sets her anchors in the wall and goes flying again, chopping off more of the Titan's fingers. No longer able to support herself, the Female Titan comes crashing down.

(Increase your **Affinity with Eren** by **1** and go to **322**.)

Who should appear but Krista?

"Jump on, everyone! Quick!"

She has two horses with her—a fresh spare, and Jean's missing mount. She must have found the frightened animal and come looking for you. You remember that even in training, Krista was on good terms with the horses. All of you mount up, thanking Krista as you do so.

"Thank goodness," she says. "I'm just… I'm just so glad that the worst hadn't happened to you." There are tears in her eyes as she smiles. She seems to be speaking from the heart.

You all feel your chests tighten to see her expression. Jean and Armin look as though they're beholding a goddess. Reiner, for his part, is obviously red-faced. You never expected to see that from someone as reserved as him.

(Go to **296**. However, if you previously heard Jean growl **"Damn!"**, go to **143**.)

●140

You decide to join the Garrison.

It's not that you were unmoved by Commander Erwin's speech, but the Battle of Trost showed you how important it is to protect the people inside the walls. (Go to **21**)

●141

The whole formation makes a major change in direction. A forest of huge trees looms up ahead of you. The "Titan Forest" is a localized group of massive trees that grow outside one wall and inside another. They can reach more than 80 meters in height, higher than the walls that protect humanity's territory.

As you get closer, the size of them becomes overwhelming; you start to get dizzy staring up at the branches.

"We're going into this forest," says Captain Levi, who has received orders from the messenger.

It seems a fresh directive has been issued to help deal with the current situation.

This tall forest was within Wall Maria until five years ago, and had been treated like a nature reserve. Wide flagstone walking paths and carriage trails stretch into the woods. They aren't in the best repair anymore, but they'll be no trouble for the horses and baggage train.

Without slowing your pace, you ride into the darkness under the vast thicket. (Go to **152**)

You notice that on the pointer finger of Annie's flailing right hand is a large silver ring.

There's a click, and a little blade extends from it. The ring has some trick to it. You hurriedly reach for it—but Annie is an instant quicker; she gouges her own finger. Bright red blood flows from the wound.

Pain: the stimulus required to initiate the transformation into a Titan.

Even as you recall this fact, there's a blinding light. Your body is blown backward by the explosion that claims your life. (Go to **14**)

"You... You really saved us," Jean mutters. "We were just tryin' to decide who... who would have to stay behind. And this loon here volunteered," he says, indicating you. "It was a tough spot."

"What?" Krista says. Her eyes go wide.

You feel a fresh wave of relief. You're glad it ended with nothing more than a tease from Jean. All thanks to Krista.

Suddenly, you realize Krista is coming up to you. She whispers: "What we talked about earlier... If I had been in your place, I think I would have said the same thing."

(Increase your **Affinity with Krista** by 1 and go to **296**.)

"So you noticed too, huh?" Armin says to you. "The commander even talked about the key to Eren's basement. He wanted someone here to hear that. Plus, the way he focused on how bad the Survey Corps' casualty rate is—he wanted to scare us more than he really needed to."

So was the idea that there was a Titan spy among them, and suspicion would fall on anyone who was willing to volunteer for the Survey Corps despite the horrible things the commander had said? That's your guess. And that puts everyone under suspicion. Wait—does such a thing as a Titan spy even exist?

"I don't know about any of that," Armin says, smiling grimly at your questions. "This is all just my speculation.

"And it's possible the spy is someone who deliberately didn't join the Survey Corps. Smart people are able to load one speech with several meanings. Maybe Commander Erwin deliberately emphasized the worst parts of reality so that only the most determined would join up."

Armin seems to be giving you his honest opinion.

But then he says, "Then again, maybe I'm the Titan spy, and I'm feeding you misinformation."

He gives you a strained smile. You can't tell if he's joking.

(You learn **Key Number Y**. Write down or remember the number **100**. Key Number Y represents the question "What can you see?" When you've done this, go back to **96** and choose another path.)

You wake up in a classroom. Jean looks to be in a foul mood.

"Dammit," he says. "That Annie, controlling the Titans—there's something fishy about it!"

"Nah, Jean. All that stuff only happened to you because you got it into your head that Annie was going to confess her love for you or something."

Everyone in the room seems tired of this. Only Bertolt looks oddly relaxed.

"Look, Jean," says Marco, the only one following Bertolt's lead. "Try not to get angry, okay…?"

"I'm gonna exterminate the Titans!" There goes Eren—again.

It's another peaceful day in middle school. (Fin)

In the scant few moments before the end of your life, you hear a screaming that reverberates in your ears. Your shaking vision shows you Eren turning into a Titan.

Perhaps your death was what gave him the impetus he needed. You pray for your friends' victory even as your life slips away.

Will Eren Yeager remember your name among all the many comrades he's lost?

(Thanks to your actions, Mikasa Ackerman and Armin Arlert survive.)

(The End / A Cruel World)

●147

You ride off to save Sasha! You've never seen such strange movement from a Titan before. What should you do...?

"Yaaaaaahhh!" Sasha cries.

You pick up the scream yourself, and end up fleeing in panic from the Titan.

"Yaaaaahhh!"

As the two of you scramble to get away, a senior soldier shows up and rescues you... (Go to **203**)

●148

You're riding along with Armin, Jean, and Reiner. Ahead of you is the Female Titan, moving at a run. You're tailing her, trying to keep a safe distance.

On horseback, the three of you talk, exchanging information. Armin tells you the Female Titan appears to possess intelligence. Jean and Reiner report that a pack of Titans attacked the right wing.

Could these two things be connected?

As you talk, something strange comes to light. Eren's position within the formation was marked in a different place on each of your strategic maps.

"So are they trying to hide things from their allies, too?" Reiner asks, frowning. "Where's Eren, then?"

"I assume he's in the safest spot in the formation, probably around the rear-center," Armin says. Reiner seems to accept this.

"Hey!" Jean calls. "We don't have time for guessing games! If that Titan's as dangerous as all that... we've gotta do something!"

He's right. If you don't act soon, the whole formation could be in danger. But a complex idea like "there's a special Titan that possesses intelligence" is too much to communicate by smoke signal.

"At this distance... I think we should be able to slow it down, buy some time," Jean says. But then, his voice shaking, he adds, "I wish." He tries to sound like he's joking, but he's serious.

The Female Titan certainly does look strong, and seems to be intelligent... The four of you together could end up crushed like insects. But maybe it would be worth it in order to protect your allies.

You're surprised. Back in training, Jean always seemed so self-centered, like he didn't care about anyone else...

"I just... don't want 'em to be disappointed in me," he mutters. Then he shouts:

"This is what we have to do right here, right now! So help me out!"

You...

Help Jean challenge the Female Titan! (Go to **223**)

No – it would be better to fall back and let the others know what's going on. (Go to **280**)

●149

You are assigned to the same squad as Jean. According to the strategic map, Reiner is in one of the nearby squadrons. This is a great relief to you. Jean and Reiner both got high marks in training.

Reiner comes across as a physically fit older brother; ever since your time as trainees he's seemed dependable. Jean is exceptionally talented when it comes to vertical maneuvering. He had a contemptuous streak back in training, but it seems to have vanished since the battle in Trost.

(Increase your **Affinity with Jean** by 1 and go to **187**.)

●**150**

The whole formation makes a major change in direction; you head into the Titan Forest. This is a localized group of massive trees that grow outside one wall and inside another. They can reach more than 80 meters in height, higher than the walls that protect humanity's territory.

As you get closer, the size of them becomes overwhelming; staring up at them makes you dizzy. New orders arrive by smoke signal and messenger. You're to dismount outside the forest and climb the trees, then make sure the Titans don't get into the woods.

It isn't just your squadron; the entire expedition appears to be splitting up to guard the perimeter of the forest.

You can't shake the sense that these orders are impossible to carry out… but soldiers who have been here longer than you are following them. This is your first expedition outside the walls; how are you to decide if your orders are impossible or perfectly reasonable? You decide to obey them.

You climb off your horse, tying the reins to a tree root. Titans don't attack non-human animals, so as long as there aren't any accidents, the horses should be safe.

Following the example of the other soldiers, you ascend one of the trees using vertical maneuvering. These plants are taller than the walls; about halfway up one, you'll already be above most Titans.

At last, the Titans arrive. They flock to the trees where the soldiers are.

There's no need to fight them. Your only job is to keep them from getting into the woods; distracting them is good enough. You might have to fight the occasional Abnormal that ignores you and tries to go into the trees, but otherwise you have little to worry about.

Still, you can't help wondering what's going on inside this forest… (Go to 151)

●151

You're on guard duty outside the Titan Forest, making sure the Titans don't get in.

Now…who's around you? (You can choose the person or people you were stationed with immediately prior to this, or you can pick a different comrade. If you do, you are considered to have been assigned a new position along with these new orders.)

Armin and Jean (Go to 256)

Bertolt and Ymir (Go to 108)

Sasha and Mikasa (Go to 172)

Krista (Go to 217)

The road runs directly through the center of the Titan Forest. The woods, home as they are to trees reaching eighty meters in height, are vast and dark. You move through on horseback. The only sound is the clopping of hooves, and even that is quickly swallowed up by the forest.

You have a bad feeling about this.

What change in strategy brought you here? The trees block your vision and make it impossible to say what direction a Titan may attack from. Eren must be thinking along similar lines, because he shouts the same question to Captain Levi.

The captain's response is blunt: "Don't ask about the obvious."

It's true; the more experienced soldiers—the members of Squad Levi—don't voice any complaints. They simply trust the orders they've been given and silently carry them out.

A sound like a whirlwind comes from behind you.

"Everyone, draw your swords," Levi says. "It'll appear in an instant."

The sound of ringing steel fills your hearing. What is "it," you wonder, even as you draw your sword.

A moment later, "it" is there.

It's running down the path through the forest at an incredible speed. A Titan, about ten meters tall. Its movements are efficient, and it has the slim build of a woman.

It's a female Titan. (Go to **277**)

She catches up to the Female Titan quickly. Mikasa draws her sword, lashes out violently again and again. Cuts and scratches appear on the Titan, but none of the wounds are fatal. The Titan appears to have the ability to toughen her skin. Nor does she stop running, even as she covers her own weak point.

Mikasa's attacks are berserk, without any of her usual clear-headedness. It's only good fortune that keeps her from being killed by a counterattack.

It looks like the Female Titan is feeling the fatigue of battle, too. She's pouring all her remaining energy into the flight from the field.

"Just wait for me, Eren!" Mikasa strikes again. Her form is impeccable.

The Titan finally stops moving for a second, striking at Mikasa with a sweeping motion of her arm.

Mikasa just manages to dodge. The tree behind her is struck by the Titan's blow, giving a great crack.

Suddenly, a new figure appears. It grabs the off-balance Mikasa from the sky.

"We need to retreat for the time being." It's Captain Levi. He must have been following the Titan as well. "We have nothing to gain by fighting now. Let's get some distance." (Go to **174**)

Finally, you hear a Titan's footsteps nearby. You and Levi move toward the sound.

The Female Titan's back comes into view, as does a soldier using vertical maneuvering around her. It's Mikasa. She must have been following the Titan as well.

Mikasa flits around the Female Titan, striking out again and again. How many attacks must she have made before the two of you showed up? The Titan is covered in steaming injuries, but none of them are fatal.

Mikasa's attacks are berserk, without any of her usual clear-headedness. The Titan spins, sweeping at Mikasa with her arm.

Oh no! you think, but Mikasa just manages to dodge. The Titan's arm strikes the tree behind Mikasa; there's a great crack and splinters come flying at you.

Captain Levi increases his speed. He grabs Mikasa out of the air even as she prepares to attack again.

"We have nothing to gain here. We need to retreat for the time being," he says. "Let's get some distance." (Go to **174**)

The Female Titan runs along, sweeping aside soldiers as she goes, closing in behind you.

The members of Squad Levi start to shout as they watch:

"Captain, give us orders! We can take down that Titan!"

"Let us use vertical maneuvering!"

You agree with them. Captain Levi's hand-picked troops ought to be able to beat that Titan. And anyway, if you all just keep running, it's only a matter of time before you get caught.

But Captain Levi says, "All of you. Have you forgotten the orders your squad received?" He looks straight at Eren as he speaks. "They're to protect this brat. With your lives. We keep riding."

At that, the squad members' attitude changes. "Understood, sir!" they say, their faces now full of unshakable resolve.

Behind you, one soldier after another flings themselves at the Female Titan in an attempt to protect you and Squad Levi. The Female Titan continues to swat them down with precise, unsparing movements.

(If the Kill Count is 1 or greater, increase it by 2 now. If it is 0, do not change it.)

Eren seems unable to accept it: not the deaths of his comrades, not the fact that Squad Levi is leaving their friends behind in order to keep him safe.

You see him raise his hand to his mouth. He means to transform into a Titan.

There's no question that if he turns into a Titan here, he could fight back against the monster pursuing you. At that very instant, soldier after soldier is being killed.

"Eren, what are you doing?!" Petra cries.

Levi speaks. "Eren." His voice is soft, yet it carries unmistakably even over the sounds of clattering hooves and raging wind. "You aren't wrong. The unit's decision is based on experience—but you don't have to rely on that. You have a choice: trust yourself… or trust me and the members of the Survey Corps."

He goes on, almost in a whisper: "I don't know the right answer. You can choose to put faith in your own strength, or to believe that your comrades are worthy of trust… Either way, no one knows what will happen. The most you can do… is choose whatever you will regret the least."

Eren appears to be thinking about this.

What do you say?

"Captain Levi is right!" (Go to **281**)

"Transform, Eren!" (Go to **213**)

"I'll trust whatever decision you make, Eren!" (Go to **253**)

"They got Gunther!" A shock runs through the members of Squad Levi.

"Eren, don't stop—just keep moving forward!"

"Head for our allies as fast as you can!"

The next instant, a beam of light shines in the forest; there's a roar, and suddenly a Titan appears.

It's the Female Titan.

What's going on? Is there another one? No... If this person has the same abilities as Eren, they themselves must have escaped in the fracas earlier, then transformed into a Titan again.

"Crap! I can't believe this!" Eren shouts. "This time I'm going to finish her!"

He seems to intend to turn into a Titan himself and fight. But then the remaining three members of Squad Levi stop him:

"No, don't! Your powers are too risky!"

"Leave this to us!"

It's Petra who cries, "Please—trust us!"

What do you do?

Try to encourage Eren by yelling at him to become a Titan (Go to **270**)

Trust Squad Levi and run away with Eren (Go to **291**)

Forget about Eren and fight alongside Squad Levi (Go to **164**)

●157

Jean, Armin, and Reiner tell you how they encountered and did battle with the Female Titan. The fact that you're all on horseback makes it hard to get details, though.

The entire unit seems to be in chaos. A smoke signal goes up, and the formation changes direction.

"We're heading toward… the Titan Forest," Armin says in surprise.

It's true: you can see huge trees piercing the sky ahead of you. (Go to **150**)

●158

You stay where you are and call to Eren. You dearly hope the sight of his comrades fighting to the death will help him resolve himself…

Mikasa and Armin both move to their respective positions. They wave, signaling to each other. They're probably just about to move.

Refer to your Battle Record Sheet. Include Marco Bott in your count.

If 5 or more people are dead, go to **295.**

If 4 or fewer people are dead, go to **288.**

You notice a large silver ring on Annie's right pointer finger.

You recognize that ring. And you remember a unique feature it had...

Now you realize what the ring was really for. If Annie is the Female Titan, then pain would provide the stimulus to start the transformation.

A small blade pops out from the ring. But you're too fast; you block it. Pain shoots through you as it pierces your hand—but Annie's plot is foiled.

Annie Leonhart is arrested.

Check your Battle Record Sheet.

If the Kill Count is 1 or more, go to **242.**

If the Kill Count is zero, go to **304.**

●160

The Female Titan gives chase, running after you.

The soldiers accompanying Squad Levi, along with those who had been chased into the forest, fling themselves at her with vertical maneuvering, but they are unable to stop her. She anticipates their movements, sweeps away their wires to limit their mobility, and dodges with her body to evade their sword attacks. Unlike a normal Titan, she seems to possess intelligence.

She doesn't even try to grab and eat any humans.

Strangely, although some of the soldiers appear to be wounded when she stops them cold, none of them, as far as you can tell, are killed.

No... Your opponent is a Titan. It's probably just coincidence. (Go to **155**)

●**161**

After that, you try to return to your unit, but it doesn't go well. You receive a strange order to head for the Titan Forest. All you can think is that your commanders have become deeply confused.

At length, you encounter some defeated soldiers.

"The center of the formation was destroyed. We don't even know if Commander Erwin and Captain Levi are still alive."

"It's not just that 'Female Titan'—the Armored Titan showed up, too!"

With your commanders gone, you are divided and conquered. Not only is the expedition beyond the walls a failure, but the Survey Corps itself has been destroyed.

You start running in the direction of Wall Rose. How many of your comrades are even still alive...?

(Bad End / Destruction of the Survey Corps)

The Female Titan catches up with you almost instantly. One of her huge feet comes at you from above.

You somehow manage to dodge being struck directly, but you tumble off your horse and land on the ground. The same thing seems to have happened to Armin.

You briefly black out from the pain. Somehow, though, you force yourself to sit up—and find the Titan staring down at you.

Her eyes somehow seem almost intelligent... and cold.

You prepare yourself for death. And yet the Titan turns around and heads off. Why?

"She's not... going to kill us?" Armin says from beside you, his voice quaking. "Do you think she... recognized us just now?"

Suddenly someone calls out. "Heeey! Armin!"

It's Jean and Reiner, both on horseback. You take a look around, and discover that your and Armin's horses are both safe as well. The four of you link up, then urge your horses on as you chase down the Female Titan. As you ride, you give Jean and Reiner the short version of everything you've been through until now. (Go to **148**)

●163

Unfortunately, you can't choose the Military Police Brigade. That's a privilege reserved for only the top ten scorers in each class. (Go back to **96** and choose again.)

You face down the Female Titan with the remaining members of Squad Levi—Oluo, Petra, and Eld.

"Hey, rookie!" Oluo spits. "Just make sure you don't slow us down!"

Well, you knew that already. You don't expect to be able to match the effectiveness of these three hardened soldiers in combat. But you believe you can do something.

The three of them form a single group as they attack the Female Titan. She bats them away with a nimble motion.

You're sure Eld, who was at the vanguard of the attack, is done for—but even as the thought crosses your mind, he dodges the Female Titan with a tremendous display of maneuvering. Oluo and Petra launch themselves at the Titan's face from just behind him. Spinning like wheels, they each slice at one of the Titan's eyes, blinding her!

An incredible combined offensive. You can only marvel.

Eld's attack was just a feint; it was a bid to steal her vision all along. The three of them haven't signaled each other ahead of time, they just all knew what to do. So this is what it means to be an experienced member of the Survey Corps. (Go to **222**)

"We've got to get away from Eren's location!" you shout to the others, and then you point your horse toward the center of the formation—the very place where Eren is.

Armin must have caught on to what you're thinking, because he raises his own voice and says, "Good idea! Let's get as far away from Eren as possible!"

Squad Leader Ness and the others look confused for a second but then maybe they get it, too, because they start riding in the same direction.

The Female Titan sees all of you, but she turns her back on you and begins running the opposite way.

"No, wait! Not that way!" Armin calls. The Titan keeps going.

"Hey! What you think you're doing?" Ness demands, once the Titan is gone.

Armin tries to placate the squad leader. "We were trying to trick that Titan. If she's really intelligent, we thought she might try going the other direction."

"Clever. So you think she understands human language?"

"I can't be sure, but…"

Squad Leader Ness and the others understand and accept what you've done. It may or may not have been your decision to make, but it seems to have worked.

"Reiner and the others are right in that Titan's path," Armin murmurs. "I hope they'll be okay."

Nearby, smoke signals go up indicating contact with Titans.

"We're going to go back up the squads that have run into Titans," Ness and Siss say to you and Armin. "You kids, head for the center of the formation and tell them about that Female Titan. Don't stay together."

The two of you nod, then turn and ride for the middle, both of you taking different routes. (Go to **227**)

●166

"Yeah. I bet she's living a nice, cushy life with the MPs right about now," Ymir says sarcastically, then she snorts. "Krista should've done the same thing."

"That's not a very nice way of putting that," Krista says.

Bertolt's expression changes. Maybe the subject of Annie bothers him.

Krista seems to notice and says, "If we survive, I'm sure we'll meet again someday."

Bertolt nods at that. Yet, looking at his face, you can't help thinking that isn't quite what's on his mind. You can just hear him murmuring:

"That's right. No matter what, we have to survive… So we can all go back to our home, together…" (Go to **194**)

When the smoke clears, the Female Titan is towering there in an unnatural pose. Something like arrowheads are lodged all over her body, connected to countless wires.

They look like the anchors used for vertical maneuvering, but much bigger. The wires are thicker, too. The Female Titan, ensconced in these thick metal wires, can't move an inch. The smoke from the shooting still wreaths the carts lying on both sides of the road.

This isn't some slapdash solution improvised in the heat of the moment—this is a specialized weapon obviously designed specifically to tie down Titans. It was ready in advance; it seems that luring this Titan here and then capturing her was the plan all along.

Did Commander Erwin really foresee all of this? The Female Titan's attack? The retreat into the Titan Forest? The fact that if Eren and the others ran down this road, the Titan would follow them straight into the trap?

The soldiers all cheer. This unit acted with Commander Erwin to have this trap ready.

"We did it! Did you see that?!"

"You get a load of that, Eren? That's the Survey Corps at work!"

Squad Levi, the unit that had been working with Eren, cheers too. Judging by the shocked expression on his face, though, no one told Eren about the weapon or the plan. It's precisely that secrecy that has garnered this extraordinary prize: a living Titan.

Captain Levi dismounts his horse, then uses his Vertical Maneuvering Equipment to get up into one of the tall trees. Standing where he can look down on the Female Titan, he appears to be talking with Commander Erwin.

The commander gives orders. Hange and Levi jump into action against the Titan. The soldiers who led the Titan here are ordered to keep watch on the immediate area; they too ascend into the trees with their Vertical Maneuvering Equipment and head to their respective stations. Squad Levi, Eren, and the others set to their work as well. (Go to **186**)

"I'll stay behind," Armin says. He's sweating, but he looks determined.

"Hey, wait just a flippin' second, Armin," says Jean, sounding desperate, but Armin goes on: "In exchange, there's something I need you to report. To Commander Erwin alone, if possible..."

Reiner listens to this, looking as worried as Jean.

Suddenly, though, Jean shouts and points into the distance.

"You're gonna tell 'im yourself, Armin. Somebody's coming this way—and they've got a horse!" (Go to **139**)

●169

You watch and wait for a time, but there's no movement underground. If Eren would turn into a Titan you might be able to fight back... What's he doing?

You...

Challenge the Female Titan yourself (Go to **218**)

Watch, wait, and pray (Go to **318**)

●170

The Female Titan comes running after you.

The soldiers who had been working with Squad Levi, along with those who had run into the forest, fling themselves after one after another with their Vertical Maneuvering Equipment, but they are unable to stop her.

She seems to anticipate what they're going to do, grabbing their maneuvering wires to throw them off course and slamming them into trees or the ground. Other times, she simply swats them out of the air or grabs and crushes them. The soldiers' blood and limbs go flying through the sky.

Unlike a normal Titan, she doesn't bring any of her victims to her mouth and try to eat them. But she does kill one person after another with precise movements. This Titan seems to be intelligent—but a cruel intelligence it is.

(Increase the **Kill Count** by 2 and go to **155**.)

●171

Bertolt, sounding oddly panicked, says, "No way. How could we drag Annie into this?"

"I'm for it," Reiner says. "Annie's very capable. It would be all right. And she knows how to turn something down if it's hopeless."

Armin, too, looks at you; he says, "I was thinking about Annie, myself. There's no telling whether she'd join us or not. All we can do is ask."

(Increase your **Affinity with Armin** by 1 and go to **251**.)

●172

You are assigned to the same location as Sasha and Mikasa.

"The long-distance enemy-scouting formation isn't working anymore," Mikasa says coldly. Sasha, for her part, seems pretty panicked. You hope she'll be all right...

For a time, you continue your attempts to keep the Titans at bay. Maybe the Titans do have some ability to learn, because they slowly start climbing the trees. Mikasa calmly dodges them, occasionally engaging. Sasha groans pathetically, "I'm soooo hungry..."

You...

Encourage Mikasa (Go to 106)

Give Sasha something to eat (Go to 276)

●173

You're in a dim forest of gigantic trees. You advance alongside Captain Levi. Once in a while he heads to the upper branches of one of the trees, as though looking for something, before deciding where to go next. And then, as if he senses something, the two of you change direction.

You use vertical maneuvering to move forward—and emerge into a clearing devoid of trees. (Go to 241)

Levi told you to get some distance. You, he, and Mikasa tail the Female Titan, keeping back a ways.

"Maybe she's getting tired, too. She doesn't seem to be moving that fast," Levi says. There's a beat, then he asks calmly, "Is Eren dead?"

Mikasa lays out her thoughts. She saw the Titan swallow Eren. If the Titan had meant to kill him, she could have simply crushed him. Deliberately putting him in her mouth and escaping seems to be her plan.

"So she may have been planning to eat him all along," Levi says. "That would mean he's in her stomach right about now."

Mikasa replies forcefully, "He's alive! Anyway, if you had done your job protecting him, we wouldn't be in this situation."

As you fly along with your Vertical Maneuvering Equipment, Mikasa seems ready to slice Levi in half.

What do you say?

"I'm sure this isn't easy for Captain Levi, either." (Go to **306**)

"Mikasa's right. You made the wrong call, Captain." (Go to **195**)

"You two aren't so different." (Go to **112**)

"We've got to get away from Eren's location!" you shout to the others, and then you point your horse toward the outer edge of the formation.

Squad Leader Ness and the others seem to see what you have in mind, because Ness says, "You're right. We risk getting cut off… but we have to protect our friends!" They set their horses running in the same direction as you. You hope to lead the Titan away from the center of the formation.

As it happens, however, for some reason the Female Titan fails to follow you. She turns her back on you and begins running the opposite way—directly into the center of the formation, where Eren is.

What's going on here? Is she intelligent enough to have seen through your plan?

"Hey! Not that way, this way!" Ness and Siss wheel their horses around and go after the Titan. You and Armin follow them.

Suddenly the Titan lashes out with her foot, kicking at the animals. First Ness, then Siss, then Armin, and finally you—with no time to dodge, you fall off your horse and tumble onto the ground.

You connect with the earth at high speed. Agony assaults your body.

When you finally roll to a stop, you fight the pain back long enough to stand up. The Titan is well away from you now. Squad Leader Ness, along with Siss, is getting to his feet with a groan. Armin is moaning; he appears to be injured.

"We're all alive, huh?" Ness says.

"Damn good luck. Never known a Titan to pull its punches before… or its kicks."

"But she's headed for the center…" Armin grunts.

"We have to worry about us first. Without horses, we're sitting ducks for the next Titan that comes along!" (Go to **115**)

●176

You're only just registering what's happening when the figure rushes at Gunther, slicing at him with a sword as they pass by!

Gunther, taken totally by surprise, has no chance to dodge. He loses his balance and slams into a tree root.

Check your Battle Record Sheet. The current Kill Count is…

Zero (Go to **178**)

1 or more (Go to **116**)

You think back... Back to the day before this meeting. Before the Military Police Brigade showed up.

You were part of a secret conference within the Survey Corps. Commander Erwin and Captain Levi were there, as were Eren, Armin, and Mikasa.

"We believe we know who the Female Titan is," the Commander said. "Our target is part of the Military Police Brigade in Stohess District. We have a plan to catch them. Zero hour is the day after tomorrow. That's also the day we and Eren are to go to the capital."

Depending on how blame is assigned for this recent incident, the Survey Corps might be dissolved; at best, its future activities would be severely curtailed. It isn't clear what would become of Eren, either.

"We've developed a plan that will make everything that's going on nice and obvious. We're staking everything on this. There will be no more opportunities."

The commander explains: Eren, being transported under guard, will leave the city and make contact with the target. They will pretend he was planning to escape. The target is after Eren, so he's going to be the bait. Survey Corps troops will have infiltrated Stohess District and will participate in the capture operation.

"It's Armin who figured out who our target is. He also proposed this strategy, which we adopted," the commander says.

You're impressed with Armin's powers of observation. But when you glance over at him, he doesn't look very pleased.

Commander Erwin continues: "The target's name is Annie Leonhart."

You can hear Eren draw a sharp breath. "What?" he says, astonished. "That's not possible. What are you playing at, Armin?!"

Calmly, Armin lays out the proof: Marco's Vertical Maneuvering Equipment. The Female Titan's reaction to the name "that suicidal bastard," which was known only to members of the 104th Training Corps.

Eren sounds ready to argue to the bitter end, but as you look in his eyes, you see the realization overcoming him. How could it not? He knows Annie well, and he fought the Female Titan himself...

"Even within the Survey Corps, only a few trusted people know about this plan. It's absolutely confidential," Commander Erwin says by way of conclusion.

The top-secret plan to exfiltrate Eren from under the noses of his guards has been put into motion, largely utilizing members of the 104th Training Corps. At the same time, however, preparations are being made for the real objective—Annie's capture. A secret plan covering for an even more secret one.

"All of you, make sure you keep this strictly to yourselves," the commander reminds you. "You can't reveal our true objective to anyone, not even your friends from the 104th."

You nod along with the others. It hurts you to have to deceive your friends, but under the circumstances you have no idea who might be a Titan spy.

The last thing Armin says to you before you go is, "When we leave this room, I'm going to act like I don't know anything about the plan, either. Play along, okay?"

(Don't forget what happened here... but go to **250** and play along with Armin.)

●**178**

Gunther is flung through the air. His arm is bent at an unnatural angle and he's groaning. He's alive, but he's out of combat. (Go to **156**)

●**179**

You all form up your squadron and advance on horseback. The formation seems to have spread out significantly; you can't see any of the other squads anywhere. From time to time, a red smoke signal goes up in the far distance, the sign that someone has encountered a Titan. Your own squad leader sends up a red smoke signal to communicate that fact to any nearby squadrons.

The squad leader says to you, "The formation's frontlines are full of experienced trackers. You newcomers are little farther back, where it's comparatively safe."

Still, Sasha looks nervous. "But what if some Titans hide out so the trackers miss them?"

You're passing by what appears to have been a village once. You see abandoned houses among the trees. (Go to **111**)

●180

At this time, if the **Kill Count is 1 or greater, increase it** by **6**. A great many sacrificed themselves to buy you this moment. If the Kill Count is zero, don't change it. When you're done, go to **167**.

●181

You hear a sound from the forest, some kind of explosion. A cannon, or perhaps a bomb…?

"Sounds like they're doing something in the woods," Jean says.

"Yeah," Armin says.

Both of them seem to have an idea what it is. Then they begin to talk.

Veering off into the woods was not a spur-of-the-moment decision, they think, but part of something Commander Erwin had planned all along. The plan was all to help capture the Female Titan… and it was kept in utmost secrecy. Most likely, there's a Titan spy in the ranks.

That would explain a lot, including the fact that no one seems to be telling you anything about anything.

"I'm still not thrilled," Jean says. "They could've let us in on it a little bit. Maybe fewer soldiers would have had to die."

Armin, however, replies, "I think the commander made the right decision. Otherwise who knows where information might have leaked out and compromised the entire plan?"

You…

Agree with Jean (Go to **198**)

Agree with Armin (Go to **219**)

●182

"You were gonna go into the woods alone?" Ymir asks, sounding exasperated, when Krista tells her as much. "Shaking like that? You'd be better off running. This isn't the time to be waiting for a retreat order."

She turns and says to you, "The same goes for you. You go into the woods, the only things that can happen are you either become collateral damage, or you get in the way."

You...

Leave Krista with Ymir and head into the woods (Go to **327**)

Take Ymir's advice and run (Go to **268**)

●183

Jean actually looks relieved at your suggestion.

"Gotta say, after the four of us survived for this long, I didn't want to have to look someone in the eye and tell them to die."

But Armin shakes his head. "No... 'Leave no one behind' isn't practical. Most likely, it would just get all four of us killed." There's a beat. "I'll stay behind." (Go to **168**)

●184

"We need to restrict ourselves to one objective," Levi says quietly. "We're going to give up trying to stop the female. We gamble everything on the hope that Eren is still alive, and try to rescue him before she leaves the forest."

Mikasa, who looked so angry a moment ago, nods in acknowledgment.

"I'll wear her down. You distract her," Levi says to Mikasa.

Then the two superhuman soldiers head for the Female Titan with a burst of gas. (Go to **243**)

●185

The battle in Stohess District may be over, but there's no time to rest. You receive shocking news: a horde of Titans has appeared inside Wall Rose.

That's the area where your friends from the 104th Training Corps are stationed. Ironically, they're there because they were under guard, except for those who accompanied you to Stohess. The Survey Corps forms a relief unit.

You join the brigade. You're going to fight the Titans to rescue your classmates and friends.

(If your **Affinity with Sasha** is **2 or greater**, go to **329**. If your **Affinity with Krista** is **3 or greater**, go to **330**.)

The capture mechanisms totally succeeds in immobilizing the Female Titan, but she has assumed a pose in which both hands protect the nape of her neck. She must have done that the instant the cannons fired. She's proving to be one tough foe.

The Survey Corps evidently intends to cut into the Titan's body and remove whatever is inside. They must think there's a human in there, just like with Eren. And if she is like Eren, then the human is resting at the nape of the neck. Perhaps that's why the Female Titan is protecting her nape so aggressively.

This means a very difficult job for the Survey Corps.

The most capable soldiers in the unit, Levi and Mike, both set to work with their swords, but they don't manage to cut off the arm guarding the neck. It looks like the Female Titan has the ability to harden that area.

The enemy may be immobilized, but you don't have unlimited time. You're outside the walls now. And where humans have gathered, Titans will come...

Commander Erwin issues an order. He wants to use the gunpowder from the capture mechanisms to blow off the hand at the wrist. It's not a subtle solution, but it might finally allow you to get at whoever is inside the Female Titan... (Go to 286)

●187

For a time, you don't encounter any Titans.

A copse of trees rises up nearby. The only sound is the clopping of your horses' hooves.

But suddenly, you hear an earthshaking noise approaching.

"Titans!" your squad leader shouts.

It's Titans, all right—a terrifying number of them. You can just make them out in between the trees. They're of the 10-meter class, and you estimate there are more than ten of them! How many more, you don't know.

Your unit dissolves into chaos.

"I know we're outside the walls, but how can there be so many at once?!"

"This has never happened before!"

The group is totally crippled. You can't find a moment in which to send up a smoke signal to alert everyone else to the situation.

"You rookies, go!" the squad leader shouts. "Link up with the other units and tell them what's going on!"

You do as you're told, whipping your horse on desperately. (Go to **102**)

●188

The path through the forest stretches on. The woods, full of trees 80 meters and taller, is dim and eerie. All you can hear are the sound of your own horse's hooves and the clattering of the wagons. And even those sounds seem to be sucked up by the dark foliage. (Go to **124**)

●189

Even your squad leaders, experienced soldiers, remark on how this is unprecedented for an expedition beyond the walls, how it warrants waiting for instructions from the commander.

"Let me go help them!" Krista begs, but the squad leaders' judgment prevails over an imploring rookie. (Go to **299**)

●190

Mikasa's face shows no hesitation. You realize she's been prepared for this for a long time now. She glances at you. You wonder if perhaps you've done something inappropriate, but then Mikasa says, "Thank you."

You've come to the bottom of the new hole. You wave at Armin across the way, signaling to him.

(Increase your **Affinity with Mikasa** by **1**.)

Check your Battle Record Sheet. Include Marco Bott in your count.

If 5 or more people are dead, go to **295**.

If 4 or fewer people are dead, go to **224**.

●191

Reiner runs past Armin, grabbing him as he goes by.

"That's got to be enough time, right?! Let's get the hell out of here!"

His shouting seems to bring Jean back to himself, for he sets off running as well. You follow them.

The Female Titan looks intently at her brutalized hand...then suddenly leaves. Most Titans tend to attack humans, but this one seems to leave you alone if you get far enough away.

"Lookit that. Big girl's just a big baby. She's running scared!"

Reiner looks relieved, but Armin, for some reason, appears shocked. The source of his astonishment seems to be the direction the Female Titan has gone.

"She's... She's heading for the center-rear," he says.

You seem to recall the center-rear is the heart of the formation, and Eren's location. If that Titan attacks them, there's going to be real trouble. Yet you can't help thinking that there may be something else behind Armin's amazed expression.

You think back on some words that didn't make sense to you at the time. Could they somehow be connected? (Go to **132**)

●**192**

You all find horses and jump on, riding through the woods.

When you emerge from the Titan Forest, Commander Erwin is there, along with your friends.

Eren's injuries are startlingly bad; he's unconscious, but it looks like he's alive. (Go to **130**)

●**193**

Eren raises a cry, a mournful howl.

He turns, maneuvering directly at the Female Titan.

A bright light shines in the dark forest, and there's a sound like thunder.

You see Eren above the tops of the trees: he's a Titan now, and he throws himself at his adversary. (Go to **231**)

•194

Things continue peacefully for a while—but then something, evidently, changes. Orders come in one after another. Word is that up at the front of the formation, the right wing has suffered a devastating blow, and the formation is in disarray.

The more experienced soldiers, having heard the report, break into nervous chatter:

"What the hell?! How could the long-distance enemy-scouting formation crumble so quickly?!"

"An Abnormal…? They say something they called 'the Female Titan' appeared, bringing a horde of other Titans with her…"

Female? Even in the Battle of Trost, you didn't see any Titans with female body characteristics. Could this be some new type of Abnormal?

All the soldiers around you appear equally shaken. Bertolt is visibly pale.

"I'm not involved in all this killing for fun…!" You hear him murmur.

(**Mark Dieter Ness and Luke Siss dead**, and increase the **Kill Count** by **5**. Go to **211**.)

●195

When she hears you say this, Mikasa closes her mouth. Levi glares at you. Then he shifts his gaze forward again.

"My duty is to protect that little brat."

(Increase your **Affinity with Mikasa** by 1 and go to **184**.)

●196

Even three elite soldiers can barely contain the Female Titan; she's that powerful an opponent. She very nearly caught Eren, who was slammed into a tree root and now appears injured.

Squad Levi doesn't have much gas left.

But that's when Captain Levi appears!

"Good work," he says. "Let me handle the rest."

He throws himself at the Titan, alone. The Female Titan reaches out her hand, but Levi shifts in midair, dodging her. He really looks like he's flying. He spins furiously, attacking. He looks like a bladed wheel.

Even the Titan's ability to harden her skin seems unable to keep up with this action. He slices a tendon in her foot, landing cuts all over and robbing her of her ability to move.

He twists again in midair, and says to you, "Retreat. We have to get Eren and the other wounded out of here before she recovers."

He sounds preternaturally calm. Perhaps it's his superhuman fighting skills and his long experience that allow him to seem so detached. Plus, his orders to protect Eren are important.

"Hrrgh… Damn it," Eren groans. "Captain Levi, you could have brought her down if you didn't have me holding you back…"

The members of Squad Levi don't seem much happier about it than Eren, but they keep it to themselves and follow orders.

You all retreat, carrying off the wounded. The Female Titan pursues you no more.

You go to where the horses are, mount up and hurry to where your allies wait.

As you ride, Captain Levi asks about the situation.

You hear Petra concluding her report about you: "That rookie saved all our lives."

Levi stares in your direction for a moment, then says, "Hmph."

(Increase your **Affinity with Levi** by 3 and go to 192.)

The formation makes a major change in direction; the command unit heads for the Titan Forest.

This is a localized group of massive trees that grow outside one wall and inside another. They can reach more than 80 meters in height, higher than the walls that protect humanity's territory. As you get closer, the size of them becomes overwhelming; staring up at them makes you dizzy.

"It looks like the wagons can manage in here," Commander Erwin says as you enter.

This tall forest was within Wall Maria until five years ago, and had been treated like a nature reserve. Wide flagstone walking paths and carriage trails stretch into the woods. They aren't in the best repair anymore, but they look useable.

"Take a message to the rear. Tell them only the unit assigned to protect the wagons in the center column is to enter the forest."

Commander Erwin issues these orders calmly, almost as if he knew ahead of time that he would be giving them.

The other units are told to position themselves around the periphery of the forest and intercept any incoming Titans.

Wouldn't that completely defeat the purpose of the long-distance enemy-scouting formation? It would represent a major change in strategy. Or perhaps the commander foresaw all this happening...?

You keep up your horses' pace, heading deeper in to the dark wood full of vast trees. (Go to **188**)

●**198**

You agree with Jean. With someone else on his side, he seems a little less nervous.

"Maybe you're even right, Armin," he says, "but I still can't let it go. We're talking about guys dying here."

(Increase your **Affinity with Jean** by 1 and go to **240**.)

●**199**

"Eren!" someone cries.

It's Mikasa, who has arrived via vertical maneuvering. She must have come here when she heard the sound of Titans fighting.

"Wait…" Her voice wavers with pain. The hint of vulnerability vanishes as quickly as it came, though. With a steely expression, she goes after the Female Titan.

You…

Are sure there must be some allies in the direction Mikasa went. You retreat. (Go to **263**)

Chase after Mikasa and help her. (Increase your **Affinity with Mikasa** by 1 and go to **153**)

You realize that this Titan is different from normal. You shout to Ness and the others not to engage her.

"What're you talking about, rookie?!"

Ness and Siss seem to be of the opinion that a greenhorn on their first expedition beyond the walls wouldn't know a Titan from a hole in the ground, but then Armin throws his weight in with you.

"I don't mean to be presumptuous, but I agree! That Female Titan is… She's intelligent. Just like Eren!"

Squad Leader Ness and Siss look at each other as they ride along. Armin seems to have convinced them to rethink things. He's a newcomer just like you, but he was with Eren at the Battle of Trost when the boy turned into a Titan. That seems to earn him a little bit of extra notice from the leaders.

And anyway, both these men are experienced members of the Survey Corps. They must realize that this Titan feels different. She's chasing you, but not trying to eat you—almost like she's tailing you, just to see what you do.

"So what now?" Squad Leader Ness says. "If she's intelligent, all the more reason we can't leave her alone. We need to deal with her ourselves, to keep the entire formation safe!"

You say…

"Let's lead her away from the center, Eren's there!" and head for the outer edge of the formation (Go to **175**)

●**201**

You use vertical maneuvering to head for where Eren and Squad Levi are waiting. They, along with everyone else, are weaving through the tall trees with their Vertical Maneuvering Equipment.

"Yeah. Sounds like we've been ordered to retreat," Eren and the others say cheerfully. "Did you figure out who the Female Titan is?"

Now you realize: only the order to retreat as such can be communicated by smoke signal. They think they're falling back because the plan succeeded. They were far enough away that they have no idea what really happened.

They're in high spirits, even bantering a bit.

Another smoke signal can be seen, not far away.

"Hey, there's the signal. It's gotta be Captain Levi," Gunther says. "Let's link up with him!"

You…

Go with them to link up with Captain Levi (Go to **257**)

Tell them what happened with the Female Titan (Go to **113**)

●202

You are assigned to the squadron under Dieter Ness. Another experienced soldier there, Luke Siss, is someone who was a help to you even in training. Armin is in the same squad as well.

You have two battle-tested senior hands, plus Armin's intelligence. It takes a load off your mind. You feel lucky to have been assigned here.

(Increase your **Affinity with Armin** by 1 and go to **110**.)

●203

The crawling Titan destroys the abandoned building, then stops moving.

You're impressed: the experienced soldiers didn't even use their Vertical Maneuvering Equipment. Nor do they bother to strike a killing blow.

"Most Titans slow down in a big way after running as fast as they can," one of them explains. "He won't come after us again, and we sent a smoke signal up, so the guys behind us will know to avoid him."

That makes sense. So this is how the long-range enemy-detection formation is supposed to work.

"This is how we deal with Normals. But if we meet an Abnormal, we'll probably have to fight it to the death." (Go to **128**)

●204

After Krista leaves, the bad news just keeps rolling in. You see smoke signals going up all around. You feel an overwhelming sensation of chaos.

Bertolt grows paler and paler. You think back on what Ymir said and try to cheer him up as the two of you ride along. Luckily, he doesn't seem inclined to do "anything funny."

At last, new orders, via smoke signal relay. The formation is making a major change in direction.

The squad leader is talking to the other soldiers. "This way is... the Titan Forest."

"Are you sure these are the right orders?"

"Yeah, no doubt. I've got them by messenger as well."

The squad leader gives the command. You all change direction, and slowly but surely the forest comes into view. (Go to **150**)

●205

There are no other soldiers atop the walls. In this situation, you're the only one who can do anything about the Female Titan.

You...

Let her go, and don't do anything dangerous (Go to **328**)

Prepare to fight the Female Titan to the death (Go to **120**)

Betray humanity, and help the Female Titan escape (Go to **290**)

An uncanny cry comes from deep in the woods. It sounds like a wild animal, but not one you've ever heard. Could it be the bellow of a Titan? Ymir and Bertolt both look wide-eyed with amazement.

Suddenly the Titans ignore you and start heading into the forest. It happens so abruptly. All you can do is watch in astonishment.

"All right, I'm going." Ymir's voice brings you back to reality.

"Huh?" Bertolt asks. "But our orders were…"

"Look at what's happening. They're going to tell us to retreat sooner or later, and if they don't, things are only going to get worse. Anyway, I'm going to find Krista."

Bertolt seems worried about what's happening in the forest, but finally he says, almost as if to himself, "It's all right… I'm sure they'll be fine… They don't need me there…"

You…

Head into the forest (Go to **271**)

Get out of here (Go to **268**)

No sooner do you dive down the stairs and around a corner than there's a shock you can feel all the way underground. You turn and see someone who was blown into the air by the impact; they're a bloody lump of flesh now, stuck to the wall. If it weren't for Mikasa's quick thinking, you probably would be, too.

"Is anyone injured?" Mikasa asks, then she shouts: "If you can stand, then run!"

All of you set off as fast as you can into the dim underground tunnel. A massive hand comes after you. Annie in Titan form—the very Female Titan herself—is reaching into the tunnel. You evade her, just in time. The hand scrabbles at the walls.

"She saw through my lie all along... She knew we were waiting for her underground. There must have been another way..." Armin says self-reproachfully in between gasps of breath.

"We can berate ourselves later," Mikasa says, calm, cold. "The question is, what do we do now?"

"Right," Armin says. "I think we should join up with the other squads waiting underground and move to plan B..."

He sounds calm again. It looks like he anticipated this possibility, and prepared a backup plan.

From down the tunnel comes a voice: "Heeeey! What was that noise? Did plan A fail?" It must be the soldiers in the other underground squads.

Armin calls back, indicating what to do next. (Increase the **Kill Count** by 3 and go to **269**.)

You bellow a warning to the members of Squad Levi. They hear you and, on the cusp of attacking, bolt away from the Titan instead. Even Eld, practically in the middle of swinging his sword, jukes away.

At that instant, the Female Titan opens one eye wide.

This was outside of any calculation. If Eld had continued his move, she probably would have counterattacked.

The Female Titan is fast. Her arms hang uselessly by her sides, but she moves nimbly on her feet, lashing out with powerful kicks. The soldiers just manage to avoid the blows.

"Thanks. You saved us," Petra says as she regains her balance and flies up next to you. "There are always individual differences in how fast they heal, so we weren't guaranteed a full minute. But we never expected her to prioritize regenerating just one eye so that she could get it back in less than half that time."

You certainly didn't know anything about that either—but for once, your instinctive caution as a new soldier may have served you well. Squad Levi, with their extensive Titan-fighting experience, might have assumed just a bit too much.

The Female Titan wastes no time. Seeing that she isn't going to take down any of these soldiers, she sets off running after Eren, ignoring you entirely. Her arms are both steaming, already starting to heal.

"Protect Eren!" Eld shouts.

"We aren't going to be able to kill her—but we have to harry her, buy time!" Oluo puts in.

The Female Titan is clever; she has more than a few tricks up her proverbial sleeve. The squad knows now that they have to be careful. (Go to **196**)

●209

Having climbed to the top of the wall, the Female Titan—Annie—stares at you with her giant eyes. Her gaze is cold, her expression flat.

She reaches toward you with one massive hand. Is she going to crush you, or take you with her...?

Before her hand reaches you, though, she stops, then jumps over the other side of the wall. She starts running, never looking back.

The attempt to capture the Female Titan has failed—Annie has escaped.

You are thrown in prison on suspicion of being a Titan sympathizer. There's an investigation, during which you undergo a very unpleasant interrogation.

A rumor you hear in the brig holds that Annie is gone without a trace. The army has yet to discover her location.

Maybe she's hiding somewhere even now, still practicing her kicks, her face as expressionless as ever.

(Bad End / Traitor's Friend)

●210

Armin is shaking and pale, but he manages to keep running. He looks at you and laughs unconvincingly. "Ha ha… That's a help. If we split up again and you go a third direction, maybe we can distract Annie just the tiniest bit."

You've come to the bottom of the underground stairs. You wave at Mikasa across the way, signaling her.

(Increase your **Affinity with Armin** by 1.)

Check your Battle Record Sheet. Include Marco Bott in your count.

If 5 or more people are dead, go to 295.

If 4 or fewer people are dead, go to 224.

●211

The squad leader and the experienced soldiers are saying: "We don't know the situation. Let's send out some reinforcements and see how things develop."

"Send me to reinforce them!" Krista says loudly.

You…

Ask to go with Krista to reinforce (Go to **228**)

Stay here, as you're worried about Bertolt (Go to **123**)

Sense danger, and are desperate to stop Krista at any cost (Go to **189**)

"I'm not smart enough to understand all this, but… It looks like he's got it rough," Connie says.

"He spent the whole time in training talking about how he was gonna exterminate the Titans or whatever—and then it turns out he's one of 'em!" says Jean. "I don't know what to think about that."

Mikasa, on the other hand, adopts a serious tone. "They must have Eren in the safest possible place. As long as this long-distance enemy-detection formation does its job, he'll be fine." As she rides along, the old scarf she wears billows out behind her. "And if it doesn't do its job… I'll go save him." (Go to **137**)

●213

You shout to Eren. In his Titan form, he's capable of helping so many people. Most of the soldiers here probably don't know about the intense fighting at the Battle of Trost. But you—you know.

For the members of the 104th Training Corps, Eren is like a place of refuge. So you shout, in the faith that he can turn this situation around.

Eren appears to hear you, because he nods.

(Increase your **Affinity with Eren** by **1** and go to **226**.)

●214

Suddenly, one of the Titan's eyes opens wide. Eld, who was supposed to strike at the final blow, is caught in her mouth. She bites down.

"She focused on just one eye so she could heal quicker?" Petra exclaims in astonishment. "Is that even possible?!" She manages to change direction at the last possible moment, but now she's hopelessly off balance.

The Female Titan doesn't let the opportunity slip. With her arms hanging uselessly at her sides, she lashes out with a kick, catching Petra with her shin. The woman is slammed against a giant tree trunk—and crushed.

Oluo is the only one left, but he's able to get behind the Titan. He launches himself at her defenseless back, bent on taking revenge for his comrades.

But his blade snaps.

As he looks at his broken sword blankly, the Female Titan whips a kick backward through the air.

It has been the work of a moment: the situation is turned on its head, the three soldiers brutally murdered.

The Female Titan had more than one trick she'd been hiding. The ability to regenerate just a single eye. Making a show of covering her nape with her hands, even though she secretly possessed the ability to strengthen her own weak point.

She's not just huge and agile. She was a better fighter than her opponents...

(**Mark Eld Jinn, Petra Ral, and Oluo Bozado dead** and increase the **Kill Count** by 3. Then go to **193**.)

You hear some kind of explosion from deep within the woods. Could that be cannons firing?

"What a noise," Ymir says. Bertolt seems oddly bothered by the sound; maybe it frightens him.

You feel a rush of anxiety yourself, and wonder what's going on. (Go to **206**)

●216

At long last, news reaches you in the Trost District Guard Unit—and it isn't good.

The 57th expedition beyond the walls ended in disaster, sustaining heavy losses. You don't know the details, but it sounds like Eren, so far from using his Titan powers to help the mission succeed, was defeated, resulting in many losses. The Survey Corps finds itself in an untenable position; Commander Erwin and the other leading members of the unit are summoned to the capital, where Eren is to be handed over into custody.

Mr. Hannes, an experienced soldier and your superior, tries to talk the leader of the guard unit into letting him testify at Eren's trial, but it is a thin hope. It's not even certain that a proper tribunal will be held.

You worry about what will happen to Eren and your friends, but as a prole in the Garrison, there's nothing you can do...

(Unhappy End / A Soldier in the Trost District Garrison)

●217

Krista is assigned to the same location as you. She ties up her horse carefully, and checks on the other animals. The horses seem to like her.

Having ascended into the branches of a huge tree with vertical maneuvering, her voice shakes with fear as she says quietly, "I wonder if the others are all... okay..."

It's just like her to put her concern for everyone else ahead of herself: what a thoughtful girl she is. (Increase your **Affinity with Krista** by 1 and go to **320**.)

●218

You leap into battle, despite having no real plan. If you can just help your comrades underground mount a counterattack...

But against the intelligent, calculating Titan, you have no chance. She grabs your wire in one hand and slams you against a building. (Go to **146**)

●219

You agree with Armin. He gives you a weak smile.

"But," he says, "I do understand... how terrible it is."

(Increase your **Affinity with Armin** by 1 and go to **240**.)

●220

You hide on either side of the road and wait.

From the direction of the forest entrance you hear several horses on the run, along with the booming footsteps of a Titan.

It's Squad Levi. Eren is there, too. And the Female Titan is right behind them. Eren is in danger!

Wait, no. They were using him to draw her out.

At that instant, Commander Erwin gives the order.

"Fire!"

There are flashes of light, roars; the smoke of explosions goes up. From the overturned carts shoot countless huge arrowheads. (Go to **180**)

●221

At that moment, you hear a voice from the woods.

"Fire!"

You recognize the voice. It's Commander Erwin.

At the same time, the forest is lit up by flashes of light and shaken by tremendous explosions. They come from just behind you, on either side of the road. The immediate area fills with smoke.

What in the world just happened? (Go to **167**)

The Female Titan, liquid dripping from both eye sockets, quickly puts one of the giant trees behind her and covers the back of her neck with her arms. Most likely, she means to protect her weak spot at the nape of her neck while waiting for her eyes to regenerate. Not only is this Titan intelligent, she knows how to fight.

Her eyes steam, starting to heal. The three soldiers, however, seem to have anticipated this. They launch themselves at her, one after another, refusing to allow any opening. They're targeting the tendons in her arms.

Chances are you have about a minute until the Titan gets her eyes back. They have to end this fight before then. This is a high-level battle conducted by experienced combatants. All you can do is watch…

The combined attack succeeds in cutting the tendons of the Titan's arms, which fall uselessly to her sides.

It hasn't even been thirty seconds yet. Victory is in sight.

The soldiers prepare to strike the finishing blow…

You…

Watch, and pray for victory (Go to **214**)

Jump into the fray yourself (Go to **109**)

ADD UP THE NUMBERS FOUND
IN THREE SURPRISING PLACES,
THEN GO TO THAT SECTION.

(Increase your **Affinity with Jean** by 1.)

Armin and Reiner agree. Despite your collective shaking, you're ready to face her.

"Let's put up our hoods to hide our faces," Armin suggests. "If she doesn't know which one of us might be Eren, she'll have to avoid killing us."

"Well, gee, that makes me feel better," Reiner says.

The four of you follow his advice, pulling up your hoods and approaching the Female Titan.

"Okay, listen up. The name of the game is to slow her down," Jean says. "If we can cut the tendons in her feet, that'll be enough. Let's not pretend we're gonna finish this fight here." (Go to **126**)

●224

You come out to the surface. A massive hand approaches and grabs you. You struggle, trying to gain even the smallest amount of time.

You're lifted through the air. The Female Titan's merciless eyes look at you.

When she sees that you're not Eren... she squeezes. (Go to **146**)

Connie smiles wryly. "She's a nut, huh? She could've joined the MPs, but she goes Survey Corps? Well, I guess I'm not one to talk."

Mikasa, her expression never changing, says, "Sasha's intuition is sometimes strikingly accurate. Usually for the worse." (Go to **137**)

●226

"I'll… I'll do it!" Eren yells.

The members of Squad Levi look a bit panicked. Only Captain Levi himself gets a small, quiet smile on his face.

Eren bites decisively into his own hand. There's a roar like thunder, and the dim forest is filled with light.

You all ride away on your horses. Behind you there's a massive impact; the earth shakes.

It's Eren, now a Titan, blocking the path of the Female Titan, who has come running. (Go to **231**)

●**227**

You're riding alone.

You see several smoke signals go up over the right wing. The whole formation seems to be falling apart.

It's hard to get a sense of your location within the formation as a whole, because it never stops moving. You waste a good deal of time getting lost, but at last you find your way to a unit at the center.

You've come to…

Squad Levi, which is protecting Eren (Go to **234**)

The central command unit, where Hange and Commander Erwin are (Go to **238**)

●**228**

You volunteer to accompany Krista as reinforcements.

Ymir looks at Bertolt, who's growing more and more pale, and says, "I'll stick with this guy. I'm worried about him."

You find this a little odd; Ymir is usually joined to Krista at the hip. But then again, there's not much room for personal feelings when you have a job to do.

You and Krista set out to help. (Go to **283**)

●**229**

You and Mikasa proceed through the dim forest, huge trees rising up on every side. (Increase your **Affinity with Mikasa** by **1**.)

You hear noises far away. Given the distance, you can tell how loud they must be. Mikasa is heading straight for them, and you follow after her.

The sounds get louder and louder. They seem to be coming from something striking so hard that even the massive trees of this forest are being broken in half.

Then, suddenly, they stop.

At the same instant, you emerge into an open, treeless area. (Go to 236)

●230

You consider climbing up the defensive barrier—Wall Sheena. It would take most of the gas in your Vertical Maneuvering Equipment, not to mention a lot of time, to climb something as tall as the outer wall. But if you don't position yourself up there, there's a good chance you would be unable to catch up with the Female Titan if she made for the wall. Granted, if she goes anywhere else, your move will be for naught...

You have the resupply squad give you more gas, then head for the outer wall and work your way up.

The only question now is, have you made the right choice?

From the top of Wall Sheena, 50 meters up, you can look out over the whole town. You see many buildings reduced to rubble. The awfulness of a Titan rampaging through a human city finally comes home to you. (Increase the **Kill Count** by **20** and go to **273**.)

Eren, in Titan form, shoves the Female Titan to the ground and holds her down. With an unearthly bellow, he moves into take a bite out of her neck.

The Female Titan grabs Eren's arm with a lightning-quick movement. She twists her body to push him away, lifting him up, then kicks him back.

Eren slams into a giant tree, but he immediately rises, winds up, and launches a punch. The Female Titan narrowly dodges it, falling on the ground. Eren, too, tumbles over with his own momentum.

Two 15-meter Titans are in front of you. You never imagined such large creatures could move and strike with such speed. The impact as they hit the ground shakes the air so violently that even you, floating some distance away, find yourself wavering with it.

As for the forest floor, it must be shaking like an earthquake. (Go to **232**)

●232

Two 15-meter Titans are engaged in a hand-to-hand battle the likes of which has never been seen before.

Eren howls, and even that is enough to shake the air. Next to these monsters, the massive trees look no larger than their average-sized cousins.

All you can do is watch this awesome combat. What could one small human, a mere rookie soldier, do? (Go to **278**)

Krista, Ymir, and Bertolt are all in the unit you've been assigned to.

You're at the very back of the formation. There are many wagons carrying supplies to support the forward troops, along with plenty of extra horses. If someone in another unit loses their mount, a new one can be sent from here.

Speaking of horses, Krista seems to have quite an affinity for them. During your month of training, not only her own animal, but many of the other horses grew to like her very much. Even the experienced members of the Survey Corps were impressed. Maybe that's why they posted her here.

You relax a little. This is the tail. If anyone's going to run into any Titans, it will be the units in front of you. Your current spot seems awfully safe...

You catch Krista murmuring, "I hope everyone's okay... I would hate for us to be safe back here while they were dealing with all the danger..." What a sweet girl. You feel a little guilty for thinking only of yourself.

"It's a little early to relax," Ymir says. "Who knows? Maybe some fleet-footed Titan will rush us from behind or something." She doesn't sound very pleased about the idea. Then she says, "And you, Krista. Worry about yourself before you go thinking about others. Outside the walls, there's nowhere completely safe."

Bertolt, for his part, is muttering something to himself. You don't blame him for being nervous: you're taking your lives in your hands on this expedition. (Increase your **Affinity with Krista** by 1 and go to **133**.)

●234

You link up with Captain Levi's squadron. Eren is here, too.

"I understand what you're saying. Stay here with my unit," Captain Levi says to you.

It seems some new information arrived while you were wandering around. One of the other soldiers is kind enough to bring you up to speed: the formation's right wing is in shambles, and the "Female Titan" has destroyed several units.

"Thankfully, no one's been killed—or so we're told. I don't know if it's true," Gunther, one of the soldiers, says.

However that may be, this unexpected development prompts the entire formation to make a major change in direction. As you progress forward, you see giant trees in the distance. (Go to **141**)

●235

"Ohh… Of all the luck… To be posted here," Sasha mutters.

You ask her what she means.

"We're 'outside the wall' in terms of the whole formation. If any Titans wander by and attack us, they'll come here for sure. Not that I'm saying I want them to attack my friends somewhere else…"

You appreciate what she's saying, but you wonder if maybe she's being a little overanxious. (Go to **179**)

There you see two 15-meter-tall Titans.

The trees around you, dozens of meters tall themselves, are bent and broken. The sounds you were hearing must have been these monsters fighting.

One of them has long golden hair and a feminine body—the Female Titan.

The other one is slumped on the ground and missing its head. Is that Eren in his Titan form?

You realize there are corpses in the area, belonging to soldiers of the Survey Corps. There must have been a tremendous battle here—but it's obviously over now.

The Female Titan appears to have won.

(**Mark Gunther, Eld, Petra, and Oluo dead.** Increase the **Kill Count** by **10**.)

The Female Titan opens her mouth wide and bites down on her defeated foe.

"Eren!" Mikasa screams from beside you. So it was him.

You take it all in: Eren's body, being ripped from the fallen Titan… and swallowed by the Female Titan.

When she has done this, the Female Titan stands up, her back to you. She runs into the forest in the opposite direction from where your friends in the Survey Corps are.

"Wait... Don't go, Eren..." Mikasa says in a thin voice, almost weeping.

But this moment of vulnerability lasts for no more than an instant. Her face hardens into an expression of resolve, and with a burst of gas from her Vertical Maneuvering Equipment, she sets off after the Female Titan.

You follow her. (Go to **153**)

●**237**

You doubt Mikasa expected a fellow soldier to interfere with her at this moment. She tumbles from the wall with an expression of shock. Halfway down, though, she fires her anchors, lodging them in the wall— but she's too late. It will take her time to scale the wall again.

With that window of opportunity, the Female Titan uses her remaining hand to climb to the top of the wall. (Go to **290**)

You head for the center-front command squadron. In addition to Commander Erwin, Squad Leader Hange is there, along with Mike.

"Thanks for your report," Hange says, nodding at what you have to say. "So there's a Titan who shows intelligence..." The researcher appears profoundly interested, but not surprised. Perhaps there had already been speculation about the existence of such a Titan.

This unit is trailing a large number of wagons. You suppose they're hauling resources for the supply depot.

Hange spots you staring at the wagons and says, "Now that you've made contact with our unit, there isn't much choice. For the sake of secrecy, you'd better stick with us."

Thus you end up joining the command unit. Information flows into it from every quarter—including news that the right wing has been shattered, and the "Female Titan" has destroyed several units...

"The reports also claim, though, that this Titan hasn't killed any humans," Hange says. "Although we can't be sure the information is correct..."

After Commander Erwin hears your report, he seems to come to some kind of decision. He issues new orders, and the whole formation makes a major shift in direction.

As you progress forward, you see giant trees in the distance.

(Increase your **Affinity with Hange** by 1 and go to **197**.)

●239

"Yeah, you're right… Maybe I can find my horse if I check the area." Jean has a strained smile on his face. "Heh. To think… We all manage to cheat death, just to wind up like this."

The barb seems directed less at you than at fate itself. (Go to **168**)

●240

"It's easy to say what should have been done after you already know the outcome," Armin says. "Maybe the commander is an unfeeling and terrible person. But he considered the possible developments and then made his choice. A hundred of the lives of our comrades? Or the entirety of humanity inside the walls? He had to decide. And he did."

Armin looks back at you. He seems so… adult.

"I haven't lived very long, but there's something I'm sure of," he says. "A person who can really change things is a person who's able to give up what matters to them. People who can't let go of anything are people who can't change anything." (Go to **309**)

You see the body of a 15-meter Titan, headless and slumped against a giant tree. Then you realize: it's Eren in his Titan form.

All around you the trees, dozens of meters tall, are bent and broken. There's a huge gouge in the earth. Did Eren transform and go into hand-to-hand combat with another Titan?

"It's the female," Captain Levi says.

But wasn't the Female Titan eaten up by the horde of Titans earlier?

"If she's anything like Eren, then it wouldn't be surprising if the human inside could escape in the confusion and transform again later."

He maneuvers down toward the ground. You follow him. The bodies of several soldiers wearing Survey Corps uniforms are there. They're twisted and broken, dead.

From there, Levi conducts a sweep of the area. There are four bodies in total. They account for the entire Special Operations Squad, Levi's handpicked subordinates. The bodies hardly bear looking at.

There was obviously a huge battle here—did they die protecting Eren?

Levi says nothing, and there's nothing you can say to him.

(**Mark Gunther, Eld, Petra, and Oluo dead.** Then increase the **Kill Count** by **4**.)

Finally Levi lands on the body of the Titan Eren. The body is dissipating in a cloud of steam, but it doesn't seem to have been long since the fight ended.

"I don't see Eren," Levi reports. "Let's go."

With a burst of gas from his Vertical Maneuvering Equipment, he makes for the interior of the forest. You follow him. (Go to **154**)

●242

You hear Annie's voice: "Haha!"

You look in her direction. Somehow, she is free of her gag.

She looks at you, her eyes strangely sad. "There's no going back now," she says. "You should realize that, if you know about me. I made sure to have a few tricks ready."

It looks like Annie had the upper hand all along. Maybe she's had these "tricks" ready since the moment you found out about her ring.

You run, desperate to get away from that place. (Go to **292**)

To watch Levi and Mikasa move is astounding. While Mikasa has the Female Titan distracted, Levi gets in close. The Titan stretches out her arm, but he spins up it, drawing his swords, slashing at her face, driving his blades into both her eyes at once. Once he has blinded her, he brings his weapons around and starts cutting her body everywhere he can reach.

Suddenly the Female Titan crouches on the ground, protecting her head with both hands. Levi doesn't slow down, but strikes at her arms, cutting the tendons.

Now her head and neck are exposed. Mikasa moves in to attack.

"No, don't!" Levi calls. The Female Titan's arm comes up with incredible speed. It nearly catches Mikasa, but Levi protects her. There's a dull thud.

Levi cuts the Titan's cheek. The mouth is open, exposing... something. A human body, drenched in liquid. Eren.

Levi grabs Eren in his arms and quickly falls back.

All of this takes hardly any time at all. You can only look on, dumbfounded.

Levi's voice draws you back to the present. "Come on, we're getting out of here!"

He's still carrying the sopping Eren. The boy appears to be alive.

Mikasa looks back at the Female Titan, hesitating for an instant.

"Fall back," Levi says to her. "Don't forget what the real objective of this operation is. Your precious friend, right?"

Finally, Mikasa nods. (Go to **244**)

●244

The Female Titan leans against one of the massive trees, not moving her arms or legs, her ruined jaw agape.

In this state, it seems as if even you could finish her off—but then again, she may yet be hiding some further strength or power. Steam rises from her body; second by second she heals herself.

You presume Captain Levi's judgment is correct. There are other Titans nearby. Right now, your priority should be to retreat and get Eren to a safe place.

Mikasa is carrying Eren now. Levi is increasing your distance to the Titan, his swords out, keeping a vigilant watch on the area.

The three of you leave that place. The Female Titan doesn't pursue you. You sneak a last backward glance at the Female Titan before she disappears from view. A clear liquid is coming out of her eyes. It's almost as if she's crying. (Go to **125**)

"Captain Levi, sir!" a middle-aged man calls out from the middle of the crowd, running up to the captain. "My daughter is in your care. I'm Petra's father." The man scratches his head as if embarrassed, then produces an envelope. "I just—ahem. I just wanted to get a word in with

you before my daughter found me. She's written me a little letter, see? Talks about how she's going to serve with you, give you her everything… Ha ha ha. It looks like the girl went and fell in love without a thought for her poor old Pa!"

Petra's father looks around, then focuses on Levi again.

"Erm… well. It's just that… as her father, I think it's a bit soon for her to be a bride. She's still so young, and she's got so much ahead of her…"

Check your Battle Record Sheet. Petra Ral is…

Alive (Go to **300**)

Dead (Go to **131**)

You move toward Eren, intending to help him. Eren, in Titan form, is facing down the Female Titan. After every exchange of blows, they back away from each other again.

Eren isn't in a mad rage; he's working in tandem with the soldiers flying around with their Vertical Maneuvering Equipment. When the soldiers manage to constrain the Female Titan, he attacks. He also seems to understand when they alert him to where the enemy is.

You try to distract the enemy in hopes of helping Eren. He seems to see you.

You're sure Mikasa and Armin must be around here, too, if they're still alive. You do your best to help bring down the foe while aiding Eren.

You think you hear two voices talking somewhere in the fray:

"It looks like Eren was able to keep control of himself this time."

"It's because I lost my head that the unit was robbed of its main fighting power. I'll finish what I started."

Could that be Armin and Mikasa? You've been fighting with such intensity, though, that it's possible you just imagined the conversation.

Eren may not be berserk this time, but even so, when two 15-meter Titans go hand-to-hand, the battle is spectacular. Their bodies slam into tall buildings, every encounter producing more destruction.

(Increase your **Affinity with Eren** by 1. All the buildings that are destroyed in this fight result in no small number of civilian casualties. Increase the **Kill Count** by 20. This collateral damage is beyond your control… Go to **307**.)

You somehow manage to get back to Karanes District. You're walking down the main boulevard.

You've dismounted and are trudging along on exhausted feet, leading an equally fatigued horse by the reins. You look around: everyone appears as pathetic as you feel. Did even half of your number survive this expedition?

The supply wagons are virtually gone. Eren is lying in one of the few that remain, Mikasa and Armin tending to him. You see he's opened his eyes. At least he's alive.

Citizens of Karanes District line both sides of the road. They seem to be there mostly to gawk.

"They went out with all that pomp—and they come back like this?" someone says.

"What the hell was this expedition supposed to do? Just waste our tax money?"

The words are cruel, heartless. What do those people know...?

Suddenly you hear another voice, a voice of welcome, coming from the crowd. You look and see two children, their eyes shining as they watch your procession.

"Wow, cool! The Survey Corps is all beat up, but they're still fighting!"

The children raise their voices in heartfelt admiration. To those of you marching along, it hurts even more than the vicious criticism of the adults.

Your comrades' faces betray the heaviness of their hearts. In the supply wagon Eren, along with Armin and Mikasa, looks at the ground, hanging his head at some memory. (Go to **245**)

•248

Commander Erwin is pulled into a different group of buzzing voices.

"I've got a question, Commander!"

"Did this expedition achieve anything to justify this number of losses?"

"Don't you care about all those dead soldiers?!"

They're reporters, come to learn the news about the expedition outside the walls. Again and again they repeat the same merciless criticisms of the Survey Corps. Commander Erwin's expression never changes; he accepts it all quietly...

The failure of this operation, compounded by your tremendous losses, does significant damage to the Survey Corps' position. You receive word that Commander Erwin and all those under him who have been deemed responsible are being summoned to the capital, and that they are to hand over Eren... (Go to **249**)

Several days pass.

Tomorrow is the day you are to be transported to Stohess District under guard.

You and the other rookies from the 104th Training Corps are gathered in the temporary barracks in Karanes District. Eren is already in the custody of the Military Police Brigade, and is confined in another room. The rest of your friends, however, are all here.

Every face is dark. The leaders of the Survey Corps are almost certain to receive some kind of disciplinary action. What will become of you new recruits? A few rookies were even summoned to the capital along with the commanders.

The MPs gave you a list of those who were selected for the tribunal. It seems to consist mostly of people close to Eren. Mikasa, Armin, and Jean are on it—and for better or worse, so are you.

Your friends are worried; Krista and Reiner genuinely seem to want to go with you, but they aren't on the list, and you have to be careful not to do anything that might make the tribunal suspicious.

"Everyone, listen to me," Armin says, coming into the room with Mikasa and Hange. "We've got a plan to help Eren escape. Commander Erwin and the rest of the Survey Corps leaders have given their approval, and they'll help us. What about the rest of you? Can we count on you?"

Shock runs through the room. People fling questions at Armin.

"Help him escape? Escape where? There's nowhere inside the walls that would be safe," Reiner says.

"It would just be a temporary measure until circumstances change," Armin says. "If Eren is taken to the capital, there's a good chance they would execute him immediately. We need to avoid that."

"Do you have some way of getting him out of Stohess, then? Or are you planning an infiltration?" Jean's question is eminently practical.

"Well… I'm hoping you can all help me think of something," Armin says uneasily. "And… I can't reveal the entire plan to everyone. I know it's a lot, asking you to help me when I can't tell you what you're helping with…"

"Can't trust even us, huh? That hurts," Reiner says, frowning.

"Heh! Fine by me," Jean says. "I don't want to end up tortured by the Military Police because I've heard your dumb secrets. Let Armin do that."

Everyone is surprised, but no one objects. You all want to help Eren. And so you set about concocting a plan to break him free…

(Go to 250. **If you know both Key Numbers A and Y, add them together and go to that passage instead.**)

"Please, everyone, help think of some way to help Eren escape," Armin says.

Your friends offer various ideas. What do you suggest?

Get help from Annie, who's with the MP Brigade now (Go to 171)

Have Eren turn into a Titan in the city and go on a rampage (Go to 310)

Have Jean act as a body double to buy time (Go to 305)

●251

You continue your planning session.

You collectively decide that Jean will dress up as Eren, while Eren will hide out in Stohess District in disguise. You'll try to get help from Annie in the MP Brigade as well. You even figure out where you'll get the disguises.

There's a lot of unknowns to this plan. It might even seem a little crazy. But you have no choice except to try.

You make all your preparations and review once more.

The next day arrives. You make a show of obeying the Military Police, accompanying the transit column as ordered… (Go to 261)

●252

The new Titan, the female one, moves with unexpected speed. Squad Leader Ness and Siss ride up on either side of her as they did with the other Titan, then place anchors in her body. They simultaneously fly at her with vertical maneuvering.

The Female Titan, however, grabs Siss clean out of the air, crushing him. Then she reaches behind herself to grab the wire lodged in her back, slamming Squad Leader Ness into the ground.

Her movements are cold, efficient. The bodies of the two experienced soldiers tumble along the ground, now nothing more than corpses.

(**Mark Dieter Ness and Luke Siss dead**, and increase the **Kill Count** by **1**.)

A shock runs through you. This Titan almost seems to be intelligent. She hasn't tried to eat her human victims, either, but has simply killed them out of necessity.

Now, the Female Titan is running at you and Armin with undiminished speed. (Go to **162**)

•253

You shout.

You're determined to bet on whatever action Eren chooses to take. Captain Levi seems to have the same thing in mind.

Eren, resolved, nods at your words.

(Increase your **Affinity with Eren** and your **Affinity with Levi** by **1** each and go to **135**.)

The group of men and women fall on Annie, trying to capture her. They pin her arms behind her back and stuff a gag in her mouth so she can't bite her hands or her tongue.

Annie struggles, wiggling her fingers. You see a large ring on the pointer finger of her right hand.

That ring...

"Run!" Mikasa shouts suddenly. She grabs Eren and Armin each by the sleeve and dives down the stairs as fast as she can. You follow her with equal fervor.

You glance back. At the edge of your vision, you can see a small spray of blood from Annie's right hand. You understand instantly: the ring had some kind of device in it. Pain is the stimulus needed to transform into a Titan.

A light erupts behind you. You hear an explosion and feel an impact.

(Go to **207**)

"He's such a weak little boy, and yet he's still alive," Ymir says, her voice laced with irony.

"Don't say that," Krista replies. "Armin is a great man."

"He's a stupid man. Why would someone as weak as him volunteer for the Survey Corps?"

"He has really sharp eyes," Bertolt says. "Sometimes he notices things I didn't even think about. And he knows how terrifying the Titans are, but he chose this path anyway." His voice is shaking as he speaks. "I think that's really impressive." (Go to 194)

●256

You're on guard with Armin and Jean.

Jean seems to be in a bad mood. You can't really blame him: you've been assigned a seemingly ridiculous task with almost no explanation.

For a while, you stay there, keeping the Titans at bay. Maybe some of them possess the ability to learn, because eventually a few begin climbing the trees. Apparently this isn't going to be a milk run. You keep distracting the Titans, avoiding the Titans… Somehow you manage to do your duty. (Go to 181)

●257

As you head towards the smoke signal, a single soldier emerges from the shadows of the giant trees using vertical maneuvering. They're wearing a Survey Corps cape, but the hood is pulled up, so you can't see their face. Could it be Captain Levi? No… (Go to 176)

●258

A blinding light fills the area, along with a sound like a thunderclap.

Something breaks through the ceiling of the underground tunnel, expanding outward. You realize that a massive body has appeared and is protecting you.

You look up. It's a 15-meter Titan: Eren. (Go to 289)

You're not sure how much time has passed when something changes. A panoply of smoke signals goes up from the right wing in quick succession. They seem to have encountered some major threat.

A single mounted messenger rides up. You can hear their report from where you are.

"We were attacked. Multiple Titans. Powerful individuals confirmed." Then, "Right wing destroyed in combat. We've lost our enemy-scouting capabilities in that zone!"

(**Mark Dieter Ness and Luke Siss dead** and increase the **Kill Count by 5**.)

Nervousness runs through Squad Levi. A messenger is sent to inform the nearby squadrons. Another volley of smoke signals goes up from the right, closer than before. The danger is coming nearer, deep into the formation...

You see another signal, this time from the front. It's in order to change directions. The command unit, led by Commander Erwin, must have intuited the danger and reacted. The entire formation makes a major change in direction.

"Hang on," Gunther says. "Isn't the... you know. Isn't it this way?"

As you progress forward, you see giant trees in the distance. (Go to **141**)

●260

Armin says, "Sure. I planned to stay behind all along." (Go to **168**)

●261

You enter Stohess District, inside Wall Sheena, watched closely by the Military Police Brigade.

Eren is in a prison wagon, and also under heavy guard. Although Commander Erwin and the other members of the Survey Corps have been relieved of their weapons and equipment, they're being treated as part of the attending detachment; the watch on them seems to be largely pro forma. At least for now.

The first phase of your plan has gone staggeringly well. Partly it's because you've done such a good job of appearing obedient, but it helps that the MPs aren't working too hard at their duties, either.

After you enter Stohess District, you find an opportune moment for Jean, in disguise, to switch places with Eren in the prison wagon. Eren runs away, using the hooded rain gear you've prepared to pass himself off as a porter.

Three other people here are wearing the same outfit: Armin, Mikasa... and you. Together, you vanish into Stohess's twisting back streets. (Go to **262**)

You're wearing the same disguise as Eren and the others, a hooded raincoat that covers your entire body, along with a large porter's box on your back. The loose rain gear neatly covers your Vertical Maneuvering Equipment. Two long scabbards, when tucked horizontally across the body, are surprisingly inconspicuous.

Once you're safely in the side alleys, Armin breaks away to make contact with Annie.

"I wonder if Annie will really help us," Eren mutters. He sounds nervous.

"If she refuses, we'll decide what to do then," Mikasa says dispassionately. "Even if she won't come with us, Armin... Armin of all people should be able to get something useful from her. Information or something."

You wait, feeling as anxious as Eren. If anyone discovers you here, all you've done will be in vain. You don't wait very long, but it feels like ages.

At last, Armin comes back. He has Annie, wearing a Military Police Brigade uniform, in tow.

"Armin told me what's going on," she says. "Count me in."

"Th-Thank goodness, Annie," Eren says. He looks deeply relieved— and yet still somewhat nervous. He seems glad to have Annie along, but not entirely trusting of her. Mikasa doesn't speak, nor does her expression change.

"Let's go," Armin says. (Go to **303**)

•263

Using vertical maneuvering, you flee the forest. What more can a mere rookie do? Fortunately, you manage to find a horse before you run out of gas. You mount up and ride off, galloping out of the dark woods at full tilt.

The sunlight that washes over you once more as you emerge from among the giant trees is a tremendous relief. The main unit, which had retreated, is there too. You make your report.

At last information filters in. After you left, Mikasa linked up with Captain Levi and they were able to save Eren. (Go to **130**)

•264

You get out of there as fast as you can.

A few minutes later, you hear a sound like thunder and a scream, and another Titan appears. Eren has transformed.

The two Titans begin to battle. You wonder whose side you should take… (Go to **289**)

Armin, Eren, and Mikasa hurry underground, but Annie stays at the top of the stairs. Is she watching for something?

You take a look, too. The stairway is about four or five meters wide, and continues at that width down underground. It's large enough for three people to walk abreast.

"What are you doing?" Eren asks Annie when he notices that she hasn't followed them. "Don't tell me you're claustrophobic."

"Yeah, that's right, I'm scared," Annie replies. "Not that I'd expect that suicidal bastard to understand the feelings of a delicate maiden like me."

Eren must think she's kidding, because he shouts, "Don't be stupid! Hurry up and get down here!" Yet Annie doesn't come.

"It's too scary. Come back up here, or I won't help you."

"What the hell are you even talking about?! Get down here already!"

"Eren, don't shout," Mikasa says, trying to rein him in.

Annie, however, says, "I'm sure it's fine, Mikasa. For some reason this area's been completely deserted for a while now."

You notice it, too. The immediate area is unnaturally empty. (Go to **266**)

"Why are you looking at me like that, Armin? It hurts." Annie's voice is strange somehow.

Armin responds with a question of his own. "Annie... Why did you have Marco's Vertical Maneuvering Equipment?" He's changing the subject. "We got our equipment together. I remember the scratches and dents on yours."

"Oh, that? I found it."

"And those two Titans we captured alive... Did you kill them, Annie?"

"Hard to say... But if you suspected me a month ago, why didn't you do anything then?"

Armin looks at Annie, his eyes wide. "I can hardly believe it, even now... I want to think it's... that it's some mistake! That's why I couldn't..." He looks at the ground. Maybe he's thinking of the things he might have prevented if he had listened to his gut. "But Annie," he says to her, "you could have killed me once, and didn't. That's why we're standing here now."

Now it's Annie's turn to murmur thoughtfully. "I know. And I just have to wonder... Why didn't I...?"

Does their conversation make any sense to you?

"Hey!" Eren shouts. "There's still a chance that you're just... telling a really, really bad joke. So come here! You can prove yourself by just coming down in this tunnel!"

"I'm sorry," Annie says. "I can't go down there. I wasn't able to become a warrior."

"I told you to stop with the stupid drama already!"

"Talk to us, Annie!" Armin pleads. "We can still discuss this!"

"That's enough. I can't listen to this," Mikasa says. She pulls off her rain gear and draws her sword. "I already cut you down to size once," she spits at Annie. "And I'll do it again… *Female Titan*."

Annie suddenly starts… laughing. You've never seen anything like it from her; she's usually so expressionless.

"Armin… It looks like you won your little bet," she says. Yet she sounds triumphant as she looks down at you. "But my wager starts here."

Then she bares her teeth, and brings her hand to her mouth… (Go to **275**)

•267

Reiner doesn't argue. "You're right, somebody has to stay behind," he says. "And I'm the heaviest. It'd probably be tough even just riding double with me. It makes the most sense."

The tension among the four of you is palpable. (Go to **168**)

•268

Before you realize what's happening, the Titans who had been clustered around the edge of the forest ignore you and your companions and head for the interior en masse.

It doesn't look like there's any point to staying here and trying to carry out your assigned orders. At length, you receive instructions to withdraw.

You and the others jump on your horses and get out of there. It looks like the other units have all left their stations as well. There's a flood of soldiers falling back from within the Titan Forest. Information filters in. You learn that a large number of casualties was suffered inside the woods. They say a horde of Titans attacked…

They managed to bind the Female Titan once, at great cost, but she escaped and attacked again. Eren turned into a Titan and fought for them, but word is that he was defeated and captured. The elite Squad Levi was, you're told, annihilated. Somehow, Captain Levi and Mikasa managed to rescue Eren… but now what?

(**Mark Gunther Schultz, Eld Jinn, Petra Ral, and Oluo Bozado dead.** Increase the **Kill Count** by **10**. When you're done, go to **130**.)

At that instant, a great noise and a shock run through the tunnel. Everything in front of you vanishes. A massive foot slams down into the space ahead of you. A pile of dust and debris is the result, the arms and legs of crushed soldiers sticking out here and there.

Annie, the Female Titan, stomped down from above into the underground tunnel.

"So, what?! Does she not care if Eren dies?!" Mikasa shouts.

"I think she gambled that he wouldn't be killed," Armin says back. "Annie is hell-bent on stealing Eren from us."

Your group is at a desperate disadvantage now. Your escape route is blocked, and Annie is above you, watching both the stairs and this hole. Even if you were to jet upwards with your Vertical Maneuvering Equipment, she would attack you the moment you did so.

"Stick close to me!" Eren calls. He raises his hand. He's going to transform into a Titan. His transformation won't explode the immediate area, you suspect. He'll modulate his body to protect his friends.

But no matter how many times Eren bites his hand, no matter that it is covered in blood, nothing happens.

"I think you need to have your goal clearly in mind to be able to transform," Armin says. You think you understand. Somewhere in Eren's heart, he's still reluctant to fight Annie.

(Increase the **Kill Count** by 3 and go to 285.)

●270

You shout to Eren. He has been hesitating, but your voice seems to resolve him.

He turns toward the Female Titan and bites his hand in midair. There's a flash of light and a boom, and then another Titan is standing there—Eren himself. (Go to **231**)

●271

Using vertical maneuvering, you head into the Titan Forest.

For the time being, you make for the center of the vast copse, where you heard that strange cry earlier. Sometimes you pause, perching on a massive branch to listen, to see if you can hear anything.

You lose track of how long you spend repeating this process.

You hear the sound of vertical maneuvering and head for it. A figure flashes among the trees. You can see a scarf trailing from its neck. It's Mikasa. You approach her.

"So you're here, too," she says, expressionless as ever.

Mikasa's good in a fight, and you're glad to have her by your side. (Go to **229**)

●272

"Hey! What are you doing to my Krista?!"

The voice comes suddenly, and almost as suddenly comes a blow from behind. It's Ymir.

You have no idea where she came from, but she has an uncanny ability to find Krista wherever she is… (Go to 182)

●273

The Female Titan knocks Eren down, then comes running towards the wall. Her speed seems to have taken even the Survey Corps by surprise.

The Female Titan arrives at the wall, and takes a great leap onto it. She hardens the tips of her fingers, allowing her to dig into the wall and climb swiftly.

Who could have imagined that she would be able to climb a wall while in Titan form?

The Survey Corps has split into two units down in the city, trying to create a net to encircle her, but they can't react quickly enough. The Female Titan is coming right up the wall you're standing on, and fast.

Check your Battle Record Sheet. Mikasa Ackerman and Armin Arlert are…

Both alive (Go to 323)

Both dead, or only one of them is alive (Go to 205)

There's some kind of explosion from the woods. It sounds like cannon fire…

A short while later, you hear something else: a bizarre cry. It sounds like a wild animal, but much bigger… Could it be the voice of a Titan?

"I've heard that sound before," Sasha says. She looks absolutely serious. "In the forest near my home… It's the cry an animal makes when it's cornered, and has nothing left to lose. I was always taught that when you're hunting, it's your quarry's last moments you have to be most careful of."

Mikasa murmurs, "Your intuition is often right, Sasha… usually for the worse." She lapses into thought for a moment, then says forcefully to you, "I'm going into the woods."

"Mikasa!" Sasha says. "Were you even listening to what I just said? If you take that forest too lightly, you'll die!"

The other girl is silent. You suspect she thinks her friends are in danger in those woods exactly because she heard what Sasha said.

You…

Get ready to run away with Sasha (Go to **268**)

Go into the woods with Mikasa (Go to **229**)

•275

Suddenly, Armin produces a handgun and fires into the air. There's a high-pitched sound—an acoustic signal round.

Apparently on cue, several men and women appear and leap on Annie.

Where were they hiding? They're dressed in civilian clothes, but their movements are those of trained soldiers.

Now, where have you been while the earlier conversation was taking place?

At the mouth of the under-ground tunnel, near Annie (Go to 312)

Down the stairs in the under-ground tunnel, near Eren and Mikasa (Go to 254)

●276

"Oh! Thank God! And thank you!" Sasha exclaims. "I didn't have any time to eat on horseback!"

You're amazed she can eat at all, given the circumstances…

(Increase your **Affinity with Sasha** by **1** and go to **274**.)

●277

The Female Titan is approaching from behind at incredible speed.

If the Kill Count is zero, go to **160**.

If the Kill Count is 1 or greater, go to **170**.

●278

The battle… The battle between these two Titans defies the imagination. Eren gives himself over to his rage, while the Female Titan appears calm, responding with quick movements. This studied craft allows her to land a punch on Eren.

Eren is just as powerful as she is, however. He winds up and punches back; the Female Titan goes flying through the air. There's a crash as she slams against one of the trees.

The Female Titan climbs to her feet again, assuming a fighting stance. Unlike most Titans, who rely blindly on their own strength, she looks like an accomplished martial artist.

Suddenly, Eren stops moving. The chain of attacks he's been launching ends. It's almost as if he's noticed something about the Female Titan, something that stays his hand...

The Female Titan, is hardly one to let such an opening slip by. She brings her leg up to head height, performing a roundhouse kick with tremendous speed.

Eren's head goes flying as if it had been cut off with a sword. The head of a Titan is the size of a small house, and now Eren's is tumbling along the ground. You assume the Female Titan must have hardened her foot for the vicious kick.

Eren's massive body collapses to its knees. The Female Titan approaches cautiously—then opens her mouth wide. You can hear a popping sound as the flesh of her cheeks tears. With her mouth open unnaturally wide, the Female Titan bites down on the neck of Eren's headless body.

You see it: you see her extract Eren's human body from the fallen Titan... and then swallow it.

The Female Titan rises to her feet, her back to you. She sets off running deeper into the woods, in the opposite direction from where your Survey Corps friends are waiting. (Go to **199**)

●279

Your actions succeed in distracting the assailants. Annie makes good use of the opportunity you've given her. She's an accomplished martial artist, after all. She throws one of her attackers, then dispatches the others with a series of kicks.

She turns to you with a sort of sneering grin.

"Did you not know? Or is this all part of the act?" She scoffs and then says, "Get clear. I'm going to run as hard as I can."

You do as she says. A light shines and a roar sounds from where Annie was standing. When the dust clears, the Female Titan towers there.

(Increase your **Affinity with Annie** by 1 and go to **264**.)

●280

"Yeah," Reiner says with relief. "That's the smart thing to do. We can't die here. We have to live long enough to let them know what's happened."

The four of you split up, each of you going to a different unit to report these events.

(Increase the **Kill Count** by **9**. Your choice may have cost some of your comrades their lives, but what else could you do? Go to **227**.)

●281

You shout your support for Captain Levi. You haven't worked with him for very long, and you lack much experience of life—it's possible you don't really understand anything. But you could feel the weight in Levi's words. He may claim not to know whether the choices he's made were right, but you're sure he could feel the responsibility he bore when making them.

You don't think his choices could have been wrong.

Eren seems resolved by your words; he nods. (Increase your **Affinity with Levi** by 1 and go to **135**.)

●282

Squad Leader Hange, wearing Vertical Maneuvering Equipment, has taken command of the situation.

"It looks like Eren was able to access his powers without going berserk this time," Hange says. "Excellent."

Jean is there, too: "Back up Eren! Pay attention to where he and the female are going, get there first, and cut off the escape routes!"

You...

Work with Hange (Go to **297**)

Work with Jean (Go to **317**)

Catch a glimpse of Levi as well (only once) (Go to **313**)

•283

(Increase your **Affinity with Krista** by **1**.)

You and Krista ride along, the spare horses in tow.

You don't see anyone for a while. Smoke signals go up here and there in the distance.

The terrain turns grassy; you see a riderless horse.

"That's Jean's horse," Krista says.

Krista likes horses, and back in training, all your horses seemed to like her. Jean's animal looks scared, but it comes up to Krista. She pats its neck and it calms down.

"Maybe Jean is nearby," she says. "If he's lost his horse, he'll be in trouble." She looks deeply concerned.

You have a bad feeling about this. The abandoned horse might mean Jean is already dead.

A smoke signal goes up not far away, the color indicating "SOS."

"Let's go!" says Krista. (Go to **118**)

•284

You're worried about Eren and Squad Levi, and head in their direction. A smoke signal ordering a retreat was sent up, but they may not know exactly what's going on here. (Go to **201**)

"I've got a plan," Armin says resolutely. "Mikasa and I split up. One of us comes out of that hole, and the other comes out of the entrance to the tunnel. Annie can only deal with one of us at a time. Then Eren can escape from whichever direction she's not watching."

Mikasa nods.

"Hey," Eren says, ashen-faced. "That's as good as sending one of you to your death."

Both of them know that, yet they each run to their place. If Eren can't become a Titan, this is your next best bet for keeping him out of the hands of the enemy.

"H-How... How can you guys fight?!" Eren yells.

"What choice do we have?" Mikasa looks back at him, just for a second. "The world is a cruel place."

You...

Join Mikasa as a decoy (Go to **190**)

Join Armin as a decoy (Go to **210**)

Stay with Eren (Go to **158**)

Suddenly, the Female Titan takes a great inhalation—and then she screams, a blood-curdling howl that hardly seems as if it could be of this world.

The soldiers around you cover their ears. What is she doing?

The scream is absorbed by the forest around you... And then, as if in response, you hear a rumbling from all around: Titan footsteps. A horde of Titans is approaching from every corner of the woods.

The Survey Corps draw their swords, but the Titans don't so much as look at the humans. They flock to the female, biting into her body, tearing her apart.

Titans would never normally do this. That noise the female just made... Does she have the power to command other Titans? And did she order them to consume her, in order to destroy whatever clues she might be hiding?

"All hands, to battle!" Commander Erwin orders. "Protect the Female Titan with your lives!" And then, Vertical Maneuvering Equipment at the ready, he leaps into the fray himself.

The Survey Corps commences combat with the crowd of Titans. Because the monsters are ignoring the humans, it's a simple matter to cut them down, but there are dozens of them. Too many to deal with effectively.

Most of the Female Titan's body has been eaten. Between the steam rising from her body and that coming from the bodies of the defeated Titans around her, the entire area is thick with white haze. Everything is blurred and distorted... (Go to **316**)

●287

You tell them you'll stay behind.

"I know someone has to stay, but..." Reiner trails off.

Jean looks down and growls, **"Damn!"**

"No," Armin says. "I'll do it. I'll stay." (Go to **168**)

●288

They burst out above ground, your two brave companions.

The earth rumbles, and a massive hand smashes them mercilessly. You can see blood and chunks of flesh go flying.

Beside you, Eren is howling. Anger and sadness: at the Female Titan, at this cruel world.

Above all, at himself.

Eren bites his hand. There is no more reluctance. The death of the friend he cherished has resolved him.

(Mark either Mikasa Ackerman or Armin Arlert dead. If you can't decide, use some method such as flipping a coin—let brutal chance decide this matter of life and death. When you're done, go to **258**.)

●289

Two 15-meter Titans appear in the middle of Stohess District and start fighting each other. Nothing like it has ever happened before. The citizens must never have imagined that they would see Titans inside Wall Sheena.

The populace is screaming and trying to flee, but their flight is altogether disorderly. Some people stand stupefied, unable to move. Unlike Trost District, Stohess has never held a mock evacuation.

Some soldiers from the Survey Corps show up. They weave through the city streets using vertical maneuvering.

"Back up Eren! This time we're not gonna let the Female get away!"

You...

Prioritize the citizens' safety and try to coordinate the evacuation (Go to 298)

Defer to the Survey Corps leaders' orders (Go to 282)

Focus on what the Female Titan is doing (Go to 311)

●290

At this time, check your Battle Record Sheet.

If your Affinity with Annie is 2 or higher, go to 314.

If your Affinity with Annie is 1 or lower, go to 209.

"Best of luck!"

You can hardly bring yourselves to do it, but you and Eren flee the area.

The three members of Squad Levi, meanwhile, put on an incredible display. You glance back, just for an instant, to see that they've immobilized the Female Titan and are launching themselves at her, landing blow after blow. They've cut the tendons in her arms, rendering the limbs useless.

Surely, that will be enough to...

But when you look back again a second later, you discover the Titan has struck back; one of the soldiers is in her mouth! The Titan takes another great leap and kicks a second squad member out of the air. That's two people dead practically before you could blink, and now she's coming right for you.

Oluo, the last man standing, slices at her from behind, but his blade shatters, and he, too, dies a victim of one of her vicious kicks. The Female Titan, without the use of her arms, just dispatched three experienced soldiers in a matter of seconds...

She must be desperate; why else would she be so ruthless and unrestrained?

(**Mark Eld Jinn, Petra Ral, and Oluo Bozado dead**, and increase the **Kill Count** by 3. Then go to **193**.)

●292

You hurriedly run away.

It's the right choice. There's a flash of light behind you, a roar and a shock wave. You're blown forward, tumbling along the flagstones. If you had been any closer, you might have been killed.

You look back from where you lie on the ground. Towering there in the middle of the city is the Female Titan.

(Increase the **Kill Count** by 3 and go to **127**.)

●293

Squad Leader Ness and Siss set their vertical maneuvering anchors in the Titan and sweep around to attack from behind. You follow them. You're not at their level, but having a third body along can't hurt.

The moment you try to approach the Titan's nape, however, a massive hand grabs you.

Titans don't have eyes in the backs of their heads, do they? And their movements aren't usually so quick…

At the edge of your sight, you see Ness and Siss, already reduced to bloody chunks of flesh. The huge fingers squeeze you, holding you immobile as the Titan looks down at you. She has the face of a woman, and her eyes display a human intelligence. Such cold, cold eyes.

The Female Titan looks at your face for just a second—and then she crushes you. (Go to **14**)

●294

Provisions that can be eaten on horseback were supposed to have been distributed for this expedition outside the walls, but when you ask Sasha about it, she replies, "I ate mine before we left. I was just so nervous…"

With a touch of exasperation, you give her your provisions. They're dried potatoes.

"Oh, thank God—and thank you!" Sasha looks at you with immense gratitude for only a second for wolfing down the potatoes.

"Hey, rookie," one of the old hands says. "Don't eat too much on horseback if you're not used to it. You'll just throw it back up."

"I would never throw up precious, precious food," Sasha says. She looks uncharacteristically serious. Maybe she's thinking back to the Battle of Trost, the terrible way the Titans ate people even though they didn't need to, finally vomiting them up when their stomachs were full. (Go to 137)

●295

"Yeah, that's right."

Eren's expression changes. Thinking of his friends and fellow soldiers—all those who have died—and seeing his companions in front of him, he seems to be resolved.

There's no more hesitation. He bites his own hand. (Go to 258)

•296

Armin and the others tell Krista about their encounter with the Female Titan, although it's not possible to talk for long while also trying to ride at a quick pace.

Krista's own unit seems to have caught wind of the confusion that now reigns over the formation. Everything is in disarray. A smoke signal goes up, and the formation makes a major change in direction.

"The Titan Forest is this way…" Armin says.

It's true: you see a massive forest rising up ahead of you. (Increase the **Kill Count** by **4** now. The Female Titan has done some damage, but you've helped keep it to a minimum. Go to **150**.)

•297

"This time we're not letting that Female Titan get away!" Hange begins giving clipped, precise orders. The squad leader seems to be a different person from the one who gives frenzied discourses on Titan research. "Capture that monster, whatever it takes!"

Hange is steely-eyed. Maybe it's because this isn't just about data, it's about the fate of humanity—or perhaps the squad leader simply wants revenge for lost comrades.

(Increase your **Affinity with Hange** by **1**. The destruction of buildings leads to no small number of civilian casualties. Increase the **Kill Count** by **20**. There's nothing you could have done to prevent this… Go to **307**.)

You decide to coordinate the evacuation of civilians. Let the elite soldiers of the Survey Corps handle the fighting.

The Military Police Brigade, supposedly the guardians of order in the city, are in chaos. Some of them have fled. All that strutting around, yet what good are they when you need them? A boy, however, one of the MPs' new recruits, is engaged in hard fighting. Evidently some of their rookies were the better soldiers after all.

You hear a religionist, some Wallist type, shouting, "This is divine punishment for defiling the walls!"

You use your Vertical Maneuvering Equipment to get to a high vantage from which you can survey the situation, then shout to the people below, guiding them away from the Titans. Sometimes you dart down to help individual citizens. You rescue one elderly person whose leg has become stuck in rubble, and save a crying child as well.

These are small things, but several other soldiers and civilians cooperate with you.

(Increase your **Affinity with Krista** by 1. Increase the **Kill Count** by **18**. This may seem like a large number, but your efforts have kept it from being any higher... When you're done, go to **307**.)

Your squad is constantly on the back foot after this. The formation falls into disarray. By the time the squad leader finally decides to send reinforcements, the formation is no longer able to function.

You take an extra horse and ride off to reinforce. (Go to **129**)

●**300**

"Agh! Dad, what are you talking about?" Petra asks furiously—and loudly. She came over when she spotted her father. She grabs the envelope, her face beet red. "Th-That's not what I meant when I wrote—Captain! I apologize for my father's lack of decorum!" She's obviously flustered.

"A bride, huh? He's right. You're definitely a little young." This smug comment comes from Oluo, who has wandered up in the meantime. "It'll be a long time before you're the kind of woman I'm looking for."

"Who asked you?!" Petra, steaming, smacks him in the face.

Blood flies from Oluo's mouth. It looks like he's bitten his tongue. (Go to **319**)

●301

"This way!" The soldiers lead Sasha to a safe place, and draw the Titan away with their horses. They ride skillfully between the abandoned buildings and the trees. Just as they intended, the crawling Titan slams into an empty building. (Go to **203**)

●302

You get on your horse and retreat with the other nearby soldiers.

You ride desperately through the dim forest. Then the cluster of giant trees ends, and with a rush of relief you emerge into the sunlight once more. You rendezvous with those among your comrades who were posted to duty outside the woods.

As the soldiers gather, information starts to come in. Word is that the Female Titan appeared again. You saw her get eaten, so what can this mean? But the information is chaotic and confused.

There's another rumor, one that shocks you: it says the elite Squad Levi has been annihilated. Apparently, Eren turned into a Titan and fought, but lost. After that, Captain Levi and Mikasa together somehow managed to rescue Eren... but what now?

(**Mark Gunther, Eld, Petra, and Oluo dead**, and increase the **Kill Count** by **4**. Go to **130**.)

●303

You're in the back alleys of Stohess District.

Annie, once a member of your training cohort and now a part of the

Military Police Brigade, is walking along with you, as are Eren, Armin, and Mikasa, who are all dressed as porters. Thankfully, there doesn't seem to be anyone around; the streets are quiet. No one seems to have noticed you yet, but if anyone does, the presence of someone in an MP uniform greatly increases your chances of getting away without trouble.

"Hey." Annie, previously silent, suddenly speaks to Armin and Mikasa. "How did you plan to get past the wall if I hadn't helped you?"

"We were going to force our way over with our Vertical Maneuvering Equipment," Armin says.

"That seems a little crazy. Anyway, wouldn't it have been easier to escape before you came into Stohess District?"

"This town has a complicated geography, and we were going to use it to our advantage," Armin says without missing a beat. "And we weren't going to just try to flee immediately. We were going to pretend to go along with them, get them to lower their guard, to buy us more time to escape."

"I see... That makes sense."

The four of you walk along, saying little. You're glad that it's so quiet here that there don't seem to be any other people around.

"There. This is it," Armin says. You've come to a stairway just off the street that leads down into an ancient-looking tunnel. "This goes into the remains of an underground city they were planning to build once. It should take us right up to the outer door."

You, Armin, Eren, and Mikasa descend the stairs. (Go to **265**)

Annie, still bound, is carried underground. The confined space will ensure that she can't transform into a Titan.

Only then is her gag removed.

"I wasn't hard enough. You and the others were. That was the difference," she says with a sarcastic laugh. "I shouldn't have let any stupid sentiment interfere. I should have just killed you and all the other humans. Then no one would have suspected me."

The leaders of the Survey Corps surround Annie.

"You're going to be placed under the supervision of the Survey Corps. If you cooperate, nothing bad will happen to you," Commander Erwin promises, but Annie gives him a spiteful laugh.

"I have nothing to say to you. What are you going to do, torture me? How very human."

So this episode concludes. You and the others succeeded in achieving your "special objective." It was extremely fortunate that you were able to apprehend and stop Annie. If the Female Titan had appeared in the middle of Stohess District, the results might have been catastrophic.

Problems remain, of course; a mountain of them. Eren's custody is by no means resolved, and the capture of a new kind of human who can turn into a Titan will no doubt make the tribunal even messier.

You don't know what will happen to Annie now. She's an enemy of humanity. Fortunately, however, she hasn't yet killed any humans. Perhaps she could be enlisted to fight on your side as a Titan, just like Eren.

Maybe you'll still have a chance to talk.

(Another End / A Sliver of Hope)

You successfully prevented the Female Titan from killing anyone. The person with whom you have the highest Affinity (including Annie herself) is happy about this and admires your excellent work.

●305

"You gotta be kidding me!" Jean says. "A double might work, but why me? Eren and I don't look anything like each other. We'll get found out for sure!"

"No," Armin says, "you're about the same height…"

Everyone in the room nods. A chorus of agreement follows:

"Yeah, you do kind of look like him."

"You've both got the same nasty eyes."

"I've always thought you looked like each other, ever since training."

"Y-You rats…" Jean doesn't appear convinced, but finally he sighs and gives in. "Fine, looks like I got no choice. Now bow your heads, because we better pray the MPs aren't very good at their jobs."

(Increase your **Affinity with Jean** by 1 and go to **251**.)

●306

At that, Mikasa closes her mouth. For a second, Levi goes silent, too, but then he says, "It's my responsibility. I'll finish what I've started."

(Increase your **Affinity with Levi** by 1 and go to 184.)

The Female Titan thrusts Eren aside and makes a run for the wall. She's faster than anyone expected, able to exploit a momentary opening.

When she reaches the wall, the Female Titan jumps up and begins to climb. She hardens her fingers so that they can dig into the stone; up and up she goes.

Could anyone have imagined a Titan climbing the wall? The Survey Corps soldiers, who fanned out in hopes of encircling her, are unable to do anything.

"She's going to get over the wall," someone shouts. "Then we won't be able to do anything!"

The Female Titan is already most of the way up. Is she going to get away?

Check your Battle Record Sheet. Mikasa Ackerman and Armin Arlert are...

Both alive (Go to **335**)

Both dead, or only one of them is alive (Go to **328**)

●308

You use your Vertical Maneuvering Equipment, desperately trying to get the Female Titan's attention somehow. You won't be able to defeat her on your own, but maybe you can offer your friends underground something, anything...

The Female Titan reaches out for you.

You hear something like a shout from the tunnel. (Go to **258**)

●309

No sooner has Armin spoken than, as if in answer, an eerie cry sounds from the woods. The piercing scream is like the call of a wild animal, but it's so loud—is it the voice of a Titan?

"The hell?" Jean asks, on edge. "Whatever that is, it doesn't sound good."

Armin murmurs, "You have to give up something important in order to change something... Maybe everyone's the same that way."

You...

Head into the forest (Go to **271**)

Get out of here (Go to **268**)

"That's a fantastic idea! Plus we could get more data on Eren!" Hange exclaims with exceptional excitement.

No one else speaks, though, until Armin says, "You're joking, right?"

It's true, if Eren turned into a Titan, the Military Police Brigade would be no match for him. But the plan would put civilians in harm's way as well, and that would make him an enemy of humanity…

"Ha ha ha! Of course it was a joke! I'm sure our rookie friend here was just trying to lighten the mood a little. You're all so serious." Hange seems to want to pass the whole thing off.

You think Hange sounded pretty convinced by your idea, though… (Go back to **250** and think of a different plan.)

●311

You watch the Female Titan's movements closely. All the time she's been fighting with Eren, she also seems to have been looking for a way to escape. She doesn't seem interested in capturing Eren anymore, or in causing any more casualties than necessary.

You…

Circle around to the outer wall (Go to **230**)

Prioritize the safety of the populace (Go to **298**)

Follow your superiors' instructions (Go to **282**)

●312

You're close to Annie when a group of men and women jump on her and try to hold her down. They pin her arms from behind and stuff a gag in her mouth so she can't bite her hands or tongue.

Annie wiggles her fingers. You see a large ring on her right hand.

You…

Hurry and get out of there (Go to **292**)

Fight the people who have mobbed Annie and help her (Go to **279**)

Jump at Annie and help tie her up (Go to **119**)

●313

Captain Levi is in civilian clothes. He's wounded and can't take part in the battle.

He watches things unfold with an impassive expression, but you see that his fist is balled up and shaking. It must gall him deeply not to be able to be a part of this.

You don't feel you can speak to him at this moment, but as he sees you make for the field of combat, he says, "You'd better not die, rookie."

You salute, then jump into the fray.

(If your **Affinity with Levi** is **2 or greater**, you may increase it by **1**. Return to **289** and decide what to do next.)

You jump on the Female Titan's shoulder. Annie doesn't stop you.

Then she jumps down from the 50-meter height, and starts running away from the wall, into the great beyond. No human alive could catch her.

"Did you think there was going to be some kind of paradise out here?"

After you pass Wall Rose, Annie returns to her human form; she asks you this question. Her cold expression and sharp glance are the same as ever.

"I'm not going to thank you," she says. "I don't have much with me, and I don't know what happens now. But... Because of you, I've been able to come home."

You flee beyond the walls, into the world she and the others inhabit.

What waits for you there? New possibilities? Or just one more circle of hell?

You don't know.

(The End / Beyond the Walls)

•315

Ness shouts, "No, you'll never be able to—!"

But there's no time. He gives orders to Siss, then says to you, "No choice now. Back us up, rookie!" (Go to **293**)

•316

Commander Erwin issues orders to the exhausted soldiers. "All troops, withdraw! Mount up while the Titans are distracted with the Female's remains! Leave all the wagons here. We'll rebuild the formation on the western edge of the woods! We're heading back to Karanes District!"

As sure and authoritative as he sounds, the words weigh heavily on the spent troops. This means failure. Defeat. Surely it's no easier for the commander to give the order that it is for you to hear it.

A smoke signal goes up, indicating "retreat." That should ensure the order reaches those standing guard and your friends assigned to various points around the woods, as well.

You...

Get on a horse and accompany the other soldiers around you (Go to **134**)

Take the retreat order to your friends stationed around the forest, and withdraw with them (Go to **321**)

Go inform Squad Levi and Eren, who are standing guard some distance away, of the situation (Go to **284**)

"Hell, maybe we can keep each other from dying." Jean smirks at you. His smile isn't any friendlier than usual. Despite his cynical words, though, he leaps bravely into battle, into the place of danger.

The fight between Titan Eren and the Female Titan is incredible to behold. When 15-meter monsters clash, the surrounding buildings suffer the consequences. Cascading rubble nearly comes down on top of you, but someone pulls you away at the last moment—it's Jean.

"Hey, keep clear. We're just cannon fodder, remember?" he says as he drags you away.

You can't help thinking how different he is from when you were in training. You and Jean stand on the roof of a nearby building, watching the Titans fight.

"It's all you, Eren!" Jean shouts. He may not sound very friendly, but it's his own kind of encouragement.

(Increase your **Affinity with Jean** by 1. All the buildings that are destroyed in this fight result in no small number of civilian casualties. Increase the **Kill Count** by 20. This collateral damage is beyond your control... Go to **307**.)

Suddenly, two figures come flying out of the tunnel, one of them from the entrance, the other from the hole the Female Titan produced moments ago.

In a single swift movement, the Female Titan grabs and crushes one of them.

In that instant, you understand. Mikasa and Armin, hoping to keep Eren safe, flew in two different directions. They must have known that at least one of them would die.

(**Mark either Mikasa Ackerman or Armin Arlert dead**. If you can't decide, use some method such as flipping a coin—let brutal chance decide this matter of life and death.)

They have both been brave and noble comrades. And the Female Titan snuffed out one of their lives without so much as flinching.

You look on, dumbfounded. A scream comes from the underground tunnel. (Go to **258**)

Levi watches all this without so much as a change of expression.

"Family, is it?" You think you see the slightest hint of a smile tug at his mouth. Then he looks in your direction. He says only, "You did well, too." (Go to **248**)

●320

For some time, you attempt to keep the Titans at bay. Maybe they have some capacity to learn, because they slowly begin to climb the trees. You manage to help Krista while also seeing to your own share of the duty.

You're not sure how much time has passed when you suddenly hear something like an explosion from inside the forest.

"I hope nothing bad is happening in there," Krista says uneasily. (Go to **104**)

●321

You decide to go find your friends from the 104th Training Corps. The retreat order has been communicated by smoke signal, but you can't be sure of anything under these circumstances, and you're worried about the horses. You seek out one of your friends to see if they need help.

(Who do you go to? Pick one person from among the four below, and **increase your Affinity with that person** by 1. You retreat with them. Go to **302**.)

Armin

Jean

Sasha

Krista

(You cannot choose Eren or Mikasa—they appear to be somewhere else, not on the periphery of the woods.)

The Female Titan comes crashing down and ceases to move.

Eren, still in his Titan form, holds her down. Members of the Survey Corps surround her and begin hacking at the nape of her neck.

At long last, everyone thinks, you'll be able to take Annie into custody.

At that moment, however, Annie's body shines and there's a rush of steam. Did she have some final power to use?

When the steam clears, Annie is there, surrounded by what seems to be a huge, transparent crystal. Inside, She appears to be frozen, her eyes closed like Sleeping Beauty.

"Dammit, that's no fair! Come out of there!"

Survey Corps soldiers attack the crystal with their weapons, but even Anti-Titan-grade steel doesn't so much as scratch the surface. Maybe this thing works the same way as the Female Titan's ability to harden parts of her body.

So Annie lies in the crystal, seemingly asleep. Hange Zoë spirits her away underground, there to keep her under close watch...

Thus, one battle at last comes to an end. Many sacrificed themselves, and although you defeated the Female Titan, Annie Leonhart is not going to be giving you any answers. She is asleep, leaving only mysteries behind her. Your victory is bitterly pyrrhic.

Thanks to these events, however, the Survey Corps finds its position reversed. The appearance of a Titan within Wall Sheena, to say nothing of the revelation that a Titan sympathizer was hiding among the Military Police Brigade, is shocking. Naturally, some criticize the Survey Corps for taking matters into their own hands, as well as for the amount of damage done by fighting within Stohess District. But the majority of people recognize that their actions prevented an even greater crisis, and that without the Survey Corps it would have been impossible to repel this latest threat to humankind.

The demand for Eren's custody is revoked, and the Survey Corps is restored to good standing.

At the same time, this places a great responsibility on the Survey Corps' shoulders: the duty to break this deadlock and take the fight to the Titans.

"We will hunt down and destroy every enemy within the walls," Commander Erwin declares to the leaders of the Military Police Brigade. "Humanity's attack on the Titans begins now."

(Your fight is over at last. Go to 324.)

At that very moment, a lone soldier comes flying up the wall from the town below.

It's Mikasa.

You thought Vertical Maneuvering Equipment wasn't supposed to have enough power to reach the top of a 50-meter wall! Looking down, though, you see what's happened: Eren, in Titan form, has carried her to the base of the wall and then flung her upward. One of Armin's ideas, you're sure. It's only feasible because of Mikasa's supreme physical gifts, and it suggests the level of fine control Eren has achieved over his Titan form.

Above all, she can do it because the three of them trust each other implicitly, so much so that they can attempt something this outrageous without so much as a practice run.

Mikasa slices at the Female Titan's fingers. Apparently they aren't hardened at the point where the finger meets the hand. Then Mikasa sets her anchors in the wall. If she can sever the fingers of the other hand, the Female Titan will have nothing to support her, and will fall to the ground.

You…

Back Mikasa up (Go to **138**)

Get in Mikasa's way and help the Female Titan (Go to **237**)

You've survived the battle. How does your adventure conclude?

If one of the following applies to you, go to the passage indicated. If several apply, pick the character with whom you have the highest **Affinity**. In case of a tie, you may choose which passage you go to. However, you cannot go to the passage for any character who is dead.

Your Affinity with Eren is 2 or greater (Go to **325**)

Your Affinity with Mikasa is 3 or greater (Go to **331**)

Your Affinity with Armin is 3 or greater (Go to **333**)

Your Affinity with Jean is 3 or greater (Go to **326**)

Your Affinity with Hange is 3 or greater (Go to **332**)

Your Affinity with Levi is 5 or greater (Go to **334**)

Your Affinity with Krista is 3 or greater (first, go to **185**)

Your Affinity with Sasha is 2 or greater (first, go to **185**)

If none of the above are true, go to **336**.

"Did I make the right choice?" Eren asks you.

The battle in Stohess District is over. Many lives have been lost, and you have suffered the shock of discovering that someone you thought was a friend deceived you all. Eren was effectively at the epicenter of everything, and it must weigh heavily on him, much more than it does on you.

By now, though, you should know as well as anyone that there are no undeniably "right" choices. That in order to gain something, we must sacrifice something else. And that we cannot know the true outcome of any choice until we make it.

You of all people may be qualified to tell him—tell him that he wasn't wrong.

After you speak, Eren nods.

"Next time, I won't hesitate," he says.

He will face other difficult choices in the future, agonizing ones.

Will you be able to support him?

(The End / Eren Yeager's Choice)

You and Jean both survive. Back in training, he was a self-centered young man; he proclaimed that he was going to join the Military Police Brigade and live the pampered life of an elite. You think of all the courage he has shown since then. Is he really the same Jean?

When you raise the subject with him, he only shrugs and responds with his usual acidity, "I haven't changed a bit. What, you think I'm all happy to go throw my life away now or something? The Survey Corps is the worst. Even now, I hate being here. It's just…"

You and Jean don't get much time to just sit and talk. Life in the Survey Corps turns out to be an endless succession of crises. First, you receive word that Titans have appeared at Wall Rose, and deploy to fight them. When that's over, you find yourselves battling Titans concealed within humanity itself. Even other humans come after you for your life.

And Jean? He takes on all these dangerous duties with characteristic ill humor. He helps his friends. He even saves you more than once.

Sometime later, he says to you again, "I haven't changed a bit." But then he goes on. "I've just… started to get used to it. At least enough that *he* won't be disappointed in me."

(The End / Jean Kirstein's Vow)

●327

"Be careful," Krista says as you go, tears in her eyes. "Don't do anything dangerous."

You head into the forest.

(Increase your **Affinity with Krista** by 1 and go to **271**.)

●328

The Female Titan climbs over Wall Sheena and runs away.

You were so close. Everyone in the Survey Corps looks devastated.

This outcome, however, has an unexpected effect. The shock of a Titan appearing in Stohess District is tremendous, and more than a few people speak out in support of the Survey Corps for driving the creature away. The damage in the district is extensive, but in its own way this stands as a condemnation of the Military Police Brigade and the softness of their defenses.

Above all else, the thought that the Female Titan is still out there, alive and well, terrifies people. The royal government and the Military Police tribunal apparently decide that punishing the Survey Corps is less important than sending these experienced soldiers out to eliminate the threat.

They return Eren to his unit, and Commander Erwin and the rest of the Survey Corps begin planning their next move...

(Better End / Flight of the Female Titan)

You successfully reunite with Sasha. You discover she's been in a certain village, protecting children who were too late to run away—without the benefit of Vertical Maneuvering Equipment, using only an old-fashioned bow and arrow. You recall hearing that she came from a family of hunters, but her bravery and initiative surprise you.

When you see her again, she looks different. She is not wearing her military uniform, but a long skirt. What surprises you more, though, are the clear eyes of a hunter she now has.

She speaks to others from her home, overjoyed to see them again. She sounds different from usual, too. Your suspect her diligent formality was partly a ploy to hide a hometown drawl.

She looks much more natural to you now. But her village was attacked by Titans. Even if it hadn't been, forests with good hunting are rapidly disappearing here within the walls.

When you ask her about it, Sasha smiles and says, "Whatever happens, wherever we go, as long as we're alive, that's enough. I've made some new friends, too. Er…" She looks a little embarrassed as she adds, "And, uh, I'm awfully hungry."

(The End / The True Face of Sasha Blouse)

You successfully reunite with Krista. This is tremendously good luck. Krista and the others were attacked by a horde of Titans led by an intelligent Titan, and spent the night in a fierce defensive action in and around an abandoned castle called Utgard. Most of the Survey Corps soldiers with her were killed; by the time a relief force arrived, her unit was on the cusp of annihilation.

Ymir, the girl who had been so close to Krista, was badly wounded in this battle. You hear she did something dangerous in order to keep Krista safe. Krista is ever at her side.

When things finally settle down and you have a chance to tell her about what happened in Stohess District, she only says, "To think, Annie kept her true self hidden from us all that time…"

Just like the other members of your training squad, she seems surprised, but where you expected this kindhearted girl to be hurt, she seems to feel something else instead.

"Hey," Krista says then. "If you found out that I had been deceiving everyone, too… What would you do?"

She's staring right at you. Her clear blue eyes and beautiful golden hair are the same as ever… And yet, she doesn't look quite like the Krista you once knew.

How will you answer her question?

(The End / The Girl Who Hid Herself)

Mikasa sits before the bed in which Eren lies, asleep. After the fighting in Stohess District, Eren returned from his Titan form and fell into a sleep so deep he almost seems comatose. Mikasa sits quietly, watching over him.

She's such a fearsome presence on the battlefield, yet here she looks like a normal girl. Eren's is the quiet, rhythmic breathing of sleep, and she looks at him with something like love.

Your other friends were here to check on Eren not long ago, but perhaps out of courtesy, one by one they've left. It's about time for you to go, too…

"The world is… cruel," Mikasa says softly.

Is she talking about all the lives that were lost in these recent events? Or does she mean Annie, who was supposed to be your comrade but turned out to be deceiving all of you? Or…

Or does she mean everything, all the experiences that have made her, forced her to become, the hardened soldier she is today?

"…and also very beautiful," she goes on.

You think back on all that has happened, and you are sure she's right.

(The End / A World Beautiful and Cruel)

Your work with Squad Leader Hange Zoë caused you to see terrible things during the battle of Stohess District. When the Female Titan climbed the wall, she tore away a part of the surface... And from beneath, you saw a giant face. Are there Titans buried in the wall? You're sure you saw that eyeball move...

"Don't let the sunlight hit that Titan! Block it with something! Anything!"

The voice belongs to Nick, a minister of the Church of the Walls. You know—thanks to the work of none other than Hange Zoë—that Titans cease to move when completely cut off from sunlight. Have there been immobilized Titans inside the wall all this time?

And how does a Wallist minister know about that, anyway? Have they been aware of the secret all along? Do they have information hidden even from the Survey Corps?

When Hange finally gets a break from overseeing the work of covering the Titan's face, the researcher turns to Nick in high dudgeon.

"We in the Survey Corps have given everything for humanity. We haven't begrudged even our own lives, if it holds out the slightest bit of hope! And somehow you knew about this, and kept silent! Do you know how many of my friends have been eaten by Titans?!"

Hange looks ready to drop the minister off the 50-meter wall, and you don't think the squad leader is just trying to intimidate him. The bright, cheerful Hange you know seems to have vanished completely.

The minister quakes with fear, but appears resolved. He shouts that he will keep his secret even if he must plunge to his death to do it.

"No, you don't have to," Hange says at last. "I was just... joking." You're almost as relieved as Nick to see the familiar Hange return.

Sometime later, you have a chance to talk with the squad leader.

"I used to act that way all the time," Hange says. "The first expedition beyond the walls that I went on, my comrades got eaten. I let hatred guide my sword after that. Hatred for the Titans, and for this whole obscene world.

"But one time I saw a Titan, this impossibly unnatural living creature, and I had a sort of epiphany. I realized that what we see and what's really there can be completely different things. I started to think... What if I found a different perspective, something other than fury, from which to view this world?"

Still, you didn't just imagine the enraged Hange atop the wall. Nor are you imagining the calm and thoughtful Hange before you now. So which one is real?

"Ahh, but don't worry about that. Come on, let's share our thoughts on the Titans we encountered this time." Hange grins broadly, then begins talking with characteristic zeal. "Ready? I think..."

(The End / Hange Zoë's Truth)

You and Armin manage to survive the battle. Knowing the secret side of recent events as you do, you were no doubt able to witness the keenness of his observations and his courage.

Some time later, you and Armin have a chance to reflect on what happened.

"Commander Erwin," Armin murmurs. "He's someone who was ready to give something up in order to achieve something important. I wonder if I could do the same."

No sooner has he spoken than he appears surprised at his own words.

"Ha ha. What am I saying? Is that… really the kind of person I want to become?"

Armin begins to open up to you. About a book he read when he was young. About his dreams of the world outside the walls. Things that could be considered heresy here within them. Although he stopped speaking of them, he has never forgotten them; they've been in his heart all this time. No doubt they were responsible for driving this seemingly frail boy to a path as dangerous as the Survey Corps.

"When I was a kid, I wanted to go outside the walls. I was sure there were amazing things out there… And now I know. I know it's not as simple as that. To make your dreams come true, you have to pay an unimaginable price…"

Will Armin give up his naïve dreaming and face reality? Or will he give up something precious in order to make his dreams come true? Or perhaps…

(The End / Armin Arlert's Dream)

Captain Levi must have formed some great expectations of you, because you end up as his direct subordinate. You and his other charges become known as "the Revived Squad Levi," and although the name brings you great pride, it also comes with a welter of confusing emotions. Can you really learn to fight like the last Squad Levi—the Special Operations Squad?

You throw yourself into your duties and training so as to live up to the name you've been given.

Captain Levi—perhaps you should simply call him Captain now—is the same as ever; expressionless, keen-eyed, and curt. But you, at least, know that there's more to the man than that.

One night, you're summoned to Levi's private quarters.

"Sorry," he says. "I need some help. This is tough alone."

He removes his coat and pants to reveal compresses and bandages. He want you to help him change them. The wounds he suffered in the battle with the Female Titan haven't completely healed even now.

You demur. You wonder if there isn't someone around who knows him better, someone more practiced in medical matters.

Levi seems to read your mind. "One of the experienced members of the Survey Corps would recognize how severe my injuries are, and how much they affect my ability to fight, and that would unsettle them. There would be no hiding it from the others. But a rookie like you? You won't be able to tell the difference between when I'm hurt and when I'm healthy."

In other words, he's so far above you he isn't even worried…

The thought depresses you a little, but you help change his dressings. Seeing Levi up close like this, you marvel anew at how toned and muscular his body is. But it's also covered in scars. Some that seem to be from years ago overlap with others that are much newer. He may be the strongest of humanity's soldiers, but unlike the Titans, humans can't simply regenerate themselves. The injuries from this most recent fight aren't completely healed yet, either.

When you finish your work Levi says, almost in a whisper, "I hate people who are weak. They're always the first to die."

The numberless scars on his body are testament to all the battles he has seen and survived.

How many comrades has your invincible captain lost to death?

He looks at you with his implacable gaze.

"Don't be one of them. That's an order."

(The End / Captain Levi's Scars)

●335

A lone soldier appears in the air just above the Female Titan. It's Mikasa.

You thought Vertical Maneuvering Equipment wasn't supposed to have enough power get this high up! Looking down, though, you see what's happened: Eren, in Titan form, has carried her to the base of the wall and then flung her upward. One of Armin's ideas, you're sure. It's only feasible because of Mikasa's supreme physical gifts, and it suggests the level of fine control Eren has achieved over his Titan form.

Above all, she can do it because the three of them trust each other implicitly, so much so that they can attempt something this outrageous without so much as a practice run.

Mikasa cuts at the Female Titan's fingers with her sword as she flies. Apparently they aren't hardened at the point where the finger meets the hand. Then Mikasa sets her anchors in the wall. With another great leap, she cuts off the Titan's other hand.

With nothing to support her, the Female Titan plummets to the ground. (Go to 322)

●336

Long after the battle, you continue to serve as a member of the Survey Corps. The fighting in Stohess District may be over, but there's no time to rest. You receive word that a horde of Titans has appeared inside Wall Rose.

You and the rest of the Survey Corps deploy to push them back. You have to rescue those who were unable to evacuate before the monsters attacked.

"The wall is ruined," one of the more experienced soldiers moans. "Is this it for humanity?" The long years of service he has dedicated to the Survey Corps seem to magnify his despair.

Your commander, Mike Zacharias, though, says, "Humanity loses when we stop fighting. Until that day, there's still hope."

You nod. At Mike's command, you mount your horse and draw your sword.

You are a soldier of the Survey Corps.

The Titans may be massive and the battles may be cruel, but you will continue to fight them.

(The End / A Soldier of the Survey Corps)

A Kodansha Comics Trade Paperback Original
Attack on Titan Choose Your Path Adventure—
The Hunt for the Female Titan
copyright © 2016 Tomoyuki Fujinami
English translation copyright © 2018 Tomoyuki Fujinami

All rights reserved.

Published in the United States by Kodansha Comics, an imprint of
Kodansha USA Publishing, LLC, New York.

Publication rights for this English edition arranged through
Kodansha Ltd, Tokyo.

First published in Japan in 2016 by Kodansha Ltd., Tokyo
as *Shingeki no kyojin geemu bukku: Megata kyojin wo hokaku seyo!*

ISBN 978-1-63236-693-1

Printed in the United States of America.

www.kodanshacomics.com

9 8 7 6 5 4 3 2 1
Translation: Kevin Steinbach
Layout: Sara Linsley
Editing: Tiff Ferentini and Paul Starr
Kodansha Comics edition cover design by Phil Balsman